The Dream Book

A YOUNG PERSON'S GUIDE TO UNDERSTANDING DREAMS

PATRICIA GARFIELD, PH.D.

Tundra Books

Published in Canada by Tundra Books,
481 University Avenue, Toronto, Ontario M5G 2E9

Published in the United States by Tundra Books of Northern New York,
P.O. Box 1030, Plattsburgh, New York 12901

Library of Congress Control Number: 2001096607

National Library of Canada Cataloguing in Publication Data

Garfield, Patricia L.
    The dream book

ISBN 0-88776-594-7

    1. Dreams – Juvenile literature.   I. Title.

BF1099.C55G37 2002   J154.6'3   C2001-903419-9

We acknowledge the support of the Canada Council for the Arts and the Ontario Arts
Council for our publishing program.

We acknowledge the financial support of the Government of Canada through the
Book Publishing Industry Development Program for our publishing activities.

Design: Cindy Reichle

Printed and bound in Canada

1 2 3 4 5 6   07 06 05 04 03 02

To Zal, who is still the "man of my dreams."

ALSO BY PATRICIA GARFIELD

Creative Dreaming

Pathway to Ecstasy: The Way of the Dream Mandala

Your Child's Dreams

Women's Bodies, Women's Dreams

The Healing Power of Dreams

The Dream Messenger: How Dreams of the Departed Bring Healing Gifts

*The Universal Dream Key: The 12 Most Common
Dream Themes Around the World*

Contents

The Craziest Dream

When you compare your dreams to what happens while you're awake, your daytime life might seem pretty boring. Have you ever had any of these dreams:

- that you were flying on a dragon's back
- that you were being chased by a vampire
- that you were eating a hot fudge sundae
- that you were being kissed by your favorite movie star
- that your teeth were falling apart
- that you were riding in a car with no brakes
- that you were hunting for the room where you were going to take a test
- that you were falling through black space
- that you were soaring to the moon
- that you were running naked down the school hallway
- that you were wearing a totally cool outfit
- that you were nearly drowned by a tidal wave
- that you were trapped in your body
- that you found an extra room in your house
- that you were talking with someone who is dead?

If you have, then you're not alone. All these have been dreamed by kids a lot like you. Welcome to the wild, weird, and wonderful world of dreams!

More Sleep, More Dreams

Your dreams are changing, big time. Those hormones you hear so much about not only cause guys to get beards and girls to get curvier bodies, but they can also create chaos in your dream life. Researchers tell us that the quality of dreams changes as adolescence begins. Nice dreams decrease. Wild and wacky dreams increase. If you start having some crazy dream adventures, you should know that so does almost every other kid your age.

During the years you are doing the most growing, you are also dreaming more. The more you sleep, the more you dream. Soon, you'll want to sleep more than you used to – you might have already noticed that you get drowsy more often. The same hormones that cause the radical changes in your body during adolescence also make you feel more sleepy than at any other time in your adult life (except during pregnancy for women).

What Is Sleep?

We spend about one-third of our entire lives in sleep. We need more sleep during times of stress. Sleep is one of our basic needs.

You need to sleep, just as you need to eat and drink, to survive. Scientists are not really sure why, but they have found that people who are kept awake for several days usually become irritable, inattentive, and irrational. (Kids are often accused of not being able to keep their temper, pay attention, or think straight – maybe you can blame it on sleep deprivation!) Animals deprived of sleep for a long time grow thin and die.

Some researchers think that sleep restores something in the body that gets used up while we are awake; others think sleep removes toxins that have built up in the body as we get tired. We know that a certain "growth hormone" is only released into our bodies during the deepest stages of sleep. This hormone helps kids develop normally, and also helps to repair tissues and heal wounds.

Our brain waves change during sleep. They shift from the fast irregular rhythm (called *beta waves*) of wakefulness to a slower regular rhythm (called *alpha waves*) as the body relaxes. Sleep actually begins when the brain sends out bursts of "sleep spindles." When you feel so drowsy you can't hold your eyes open and you begin to nod off while reading or watching TV, your brain is producing sleep spindles. You may notice wisps of dreams as you drift, or suddenly startle awake before falling asleep again. The brain waves get even slower (*delta waves*) as we enter deep sleep. The slowest waves our brains produce (*theta waves*) may appear next. Your soundest sleep is often during the first hour or so of the night.

Then, about ninety minutes into the sleep period, your eyes start to dart back and forth under your closed lids in rapid eye movement, or REM. That's the dream state, not the band! This brain pattern resembles the waking waves of an active mind, but it differs because your body remains deeply relaxed. It seems like the large muscles in your legs and arms are paralyzed, while the small muscles in your face and fingers may twitch.

What Are Dreams?

When you close your eyes to the outer world in sleep, you open your mind to an inner world of dreams. Dreams are a kind of thinking that takes place during sleep. This thinking is mostly in images, like a language of pictures.

Dreaming is one of your body's basic rhythms. Throughout day and night your body temperature varies, reaching peaks of highs and valleys of lows. Your food is digested and your heart pumps your blood in patterns that increase and decrease. During waking hours, you daydream in a cycle that lasts about ninety minutes. While you sleep, you dream in the same ninety-minute rhythm. In the "low" period of sleep, you have thoughtlike dreams that are not as vivid or active as the mountain peaks of your REM dreams.

With each cycle of dreaming, you dream for a longer time. At the beginning of the night, a dream lasts only ten minutes or so. By the end of the night, you are spending 30 to 45 minutes, even an hour, in a dream. As your dream periods grow longer, your deep sleep periods get shorter. Most adults dream 20 to 25 percent of the time they are asleep. You will go through four or five REM cycles during a typical night. If you sleep eight hours, you'll dream two full hours of that time.

Dreaming through the Centuries

People have always been fascinated with dreams. Since the first written record was scratched into clay tablets in the days of the ancient Sumerian people, dreams have been part of humankind's history. If you know the Old Testament of the Bible, you might remember Joseph's interpretation of Pharaoh's dream of the seven fat and seven lean cattle, and Jacob's dream of the ladder reaching to heaven. The mother of the Buddha, the prophet Mohammed, and the founder of Mormonism, Joseph Smith, are among the people who have had important dreams recorded in holy books. Each religion has inscribed the dreams of their founders and chief followers, finding inspiration, warnings of danger, and guidance in them. Dreams were believed to be messages from the gods – and still are in some cultures.

All people have been fascinated with the mystery of dreams. Most cultures have developed ways to protect sleeping people from the evil spirits thought to bring bad dreams, and to insure good dreams. Some Aboriginal people of North America used to hang dreamcatchers above the cradleboards of sleeping infants to screen out nightmares and allow the passage of good dreams. Chinese parents provided their children with double-headed tiger pillows to scare off evil spirits who might approach from any direction. Japanese people carried amulets carved from ivory in the shape of a mythological creature called a Baku, who was supposed to eat bad dreams. Europeans hung a stone with a natural hole on a red ribbon and tied it to a bedpost to protect the sleeper.

Some societies believe that dreams foretell the future. Certainly some people experience dreams that seem to give information the dreamer could not have known in any other way. We don't really know how many people have predictive dreams and how accurate they are. What we do know is that dreams are definitely a way to learn more about ourselves. From our dreams we can find out how to make waking life better.

Discover Yourself as You Dream

This book will show you what dreams you can expect and what they frequently mean. You'll see that dreams can sometimes be shaped and you'll learn how to cope with fearful figures in your dreams. You'll get guidelines for having happier dream adventures.

How do I know that your dreams can help you? I have done several studies on dreams with people of different ages and in different cultures. Throughout this book, you will find kids describing their dreams in their own words. They have recorded their dreams for an Internet survey, and have told them to me during personal interviews.

In addition, since I was fourteen I have been recording my dreams in a journal, along with the main activities of my day. By keeping a dream journal, I learned a lot about how the dreaming mind works and how I could improve my dream life and my waking life. Although my work about dreaming has taught me much, I learned the most about myself from my own dream records. So can you. See chapter 15 "Be a Dream Detective" for tips on getting a good sleep, remembering your dreams, and learning from them.

Your dreams can teach you how you are truly feeling about yourself, your parents and other family members, friends, classmates, and teachers. They can tell you how you feel about your body. They can show you how you feel about the role you are playing in life at the moment. They can help you form your own identity.

A lot is going on in your waking life right now. You're figuring out who you are and who you want to be. You're testing your independence while still holding on to security. You're thinking about what you might want in romance and relationships. You're developing skills and pride in your accomplishments. You are finding your way to self-confidence. You're deciding what is really important in life.

Dreams can help you with all of this, and more. As you start your own dream journal, or think about and explore your own dreams, you will be expanding your self-knowledge. Your best guide is as near as your pillow. Turn out the lights. Curl up in bed. Dream and discover yourself.

1

Oh No, It's After Me!

"I go to this school for a dance or something. This guy shows up, and he starts doing things, ruining things, hurting people, and I can't stop him for some reason – either he threatens someone I like or me. So then I take off and he's chasing me. I jump into a small blue pick-up truck through the back window. I get away. [The truck] stops, and I have to make a run for it. Well, he is on a bike now! A little girly bike with a basket on the front. So I'm running and I go into this backyard, and I'm going to climb the terrace to the second floor. It reminds me of an old-style house, like the bike. While I'm up there climbing I see the bike roll by, so I know he knows where I am. So I gotta hurry, but I'm still not climbing fast enough, and sooner than it should have been, he is there, and grabs my foot, but not as a human anymore. It is a 'bad' hand."

– Jason, 15

Being chased and attacked in a dream is the universal nightmare. In every bed, in every land, people of every age dream that they see or hear or sense the attacker. We run or try to escape; we hide and are found; it comes after us, gaining on us, until – at the most terror-stricken moment – we awaken.

Jason's nightmare is typical of this kind of dream. No matter what is in pursuit, the dreamer wants to get away from it fast. In Jason's dream, the bad guy soon catches up and grabs hold of his foot as he climbs to escape. Things get worse, with the human hand turning inhuman, animal-like and evil. In most dreams like this, intense fear jars the dreamer awake at this point. Whether it's the wolf's fang about to sink into our skin, the intruder's knife penetrating our flesh, the shark about to swallow us, or the evil force overpower us, we want out of the dream – now.

You are almost certain to have this nightmare at some time in your life. Nearly 80 percent of the 100 kids surveyed said they had dreamed about being chased or attacked. Slightly more than 80 percent of adults reported having the same dream. Being chased or attacked is also the most frequent dream that children have.

As common as nightmares of being chased and attacked are, few people realize that these dreams are packed with information that can teach us about ourselves. We can learn from them and improve our waking life. Each dream enemy has something to tell us. The power of our dream villains can help us rather than harm us. Nightmares, when properly understood, empower us.

Dream Villains

Bad dreams about being chased or attacked by wild beasts or violent people may have begun in our distant past, when the threat of being pursued by savage animals or enemy tribes was a daily danger. Today, we are more likely to feel threatened by an angry parent, a critical teacher, a bully at school, a mean classmate, a vengeful ex-boyfriend or ex-girlfriend, or a jealous sister or brother.

Your feelings about these people – often relatives, teachers, bosses, or friends – may give them ferocious shapes in your dreams. Are you struggling with a difficult social situation at school? Is one of your parents seriously ill? Has there been a divorce or death in your family? Do you feel unfairly treated? These waking-life circumstances and your reactions to them can take on fearful forms in a nightmare. Dreams exaggerate and dramatize our feelings.

❋

To be chased or attacked in a dream is to
feel an emotional threat in waking life.

❋

Who or what is currently making you feel worried or afraid? The clues to answer this question are found by examining your dream:

1. Who or what is after you?
2. What are the characteristics of the villain you noticed (size, shape, color, hair, skin, teeth or claws, weapon)?
3. Who does it remind you of?
4. What does it do or try to do to you?

5. How do you react?

6. How does the dream end?

Your dream enemies may look like strangers, animals, supernatural creatures, imaginary beings, an "evil force," someone you know, or even an unusual object.

For young children, the most common dream enemy is a wild animal. Children have many more dreams with animals than adults – some researchers find 60 percent compared to 7 percent in adults' dreams. In the dreams of young children, most of the animals are dangerous.

For older kids like you, ferocious animals are still a problem, but strange men are worse. In adults' dreams, the enemy is most often a bad stranger, usually a male.

The Evil Stranger

For both kids and adults, 40 percent of dream villains are male strangers. Here are some typical examples kids describe from their dreams:

- I am attacked by a serial killer.
- A man with a knife invades my home.
- A psychotic ax murderer is after me.
- A thief breaks into the house.
- A man in dreadlocks is trying to kill me.
- I'm chased by a man who wants to kill little children.
- Boys with needles are killing people by injection.
- I'm chased by a really big person around a table.

- A man in black in a boat shoots me with a gun and hits me in the head twice.
- Barbarian soldiers on horses are chasing me.
- Enemy knights try to kill me and my family.
- Scary-looking dudes are beating people.
- Evil persons are after me.

Whatever area of your life is unknown, dark, or threatening can take the form of an evil stranger in your dream. When you are ready and able to confront your fear, the mask drops and the person underneath can be identified.

For some teens, the unknown possibly dangerous area of their lives has to do with sex. Fifteen-year-old Lisa had a classic dream of this type. In it, a boy and girl are walking up the road hand in hand. Suddenly a whip cracks and they separate. Standing between them is a tall masked stranger in a long black cape. He starts setting off firecrackers and cracking sparks with his whip. Lisa was attracted to the stranger, but was worried about the damage his whip could do. This dream expressed her growing romantic attraction in the sparks and explosions of firecrackers. At the same time the dream showed her fear of getting close.

Many teenage girls share the same mixed feelings. They dream about men with knives, swords, batons, rifles, and other weapons breaking into their homes and hurting them. These dreams may suggest a fear of getting romantically involved with boys, or they might reflect a more general anxiety. If you have dreams like this, you probably know which is more likely for you.

Oh No, It's After Me!

The Savage Beast

Your dream enemy may take the shape of a ferocious or poisonous animal, or an animal that is usually harmless but seems fierce in the dream. The savage beast may attack in a group of wild animals, or be a single "hairy creature." In my studies, animal enemies appear about the same amount in the dreams of kids (21 percent) as in the dreams of adults (25 percent).

A whole range of creatures roam dreamscapes:

- I'm chased by spiders.
- I'm pursued by wolves.
- An eagle-vampire-like monster is after me.
- Bears are chasing me down a long road.
- I'm chased by a cat outside my home.
- A family of chimps is after me.
- Doberman pinschers chase me.
- Two foxes come after me.
- I'm chased by a blue-green lion.
- Vicious wolves are attacking me.
- I'm ripped apart and eaten by a shark.

Animals in dreams usually represent wild emotions or impulses. In the list of examples, notice how often the animals have sharp teeth. Teeth are often associated with anger that dreamers feel directed toward them. Maybe Mom lost her temper and said hurtful things during the day. Or Dad, your teacher, or someone you like said mean things to you. Sometimes teeth in a dream stand for the dreamer's own anger that is barely in control.

Think about whether someone has been angry with you recently. Do you feel ready to lose control of your temper? Remember that angry words can "bite" and hurt as they leave the mouth and reach the ears of someone.

Dream Wounds Reveal Real Wounds
Physical wounds in dreams almost always represent emotional wounds in the waking state. That slash in your side from a dream shark might stand for the nasty things a former best friend said to you. The dream bear that tears at you with its claws could be sharp words that stung in a quarrel with your mother. The dream wolves that tear at your flesh could stand for the pack of mean classmates who made fun of you recently. The bee stings or spider bites in your dreams often stand for the pain of "poisonous" words aimed at you while you are awake.

The same principle applies to dreams involving people who injure you. Damage by a weapon in a dream – knife wounds, gunshot wounds, cuts from an ax or sword, bruises from sticks – can represent emotional hurts you've sustained in the daytime. Or they may express your fear of being damaged in a relationship.

But sometimes the pain of a dream wound comes from a change in your physical body. This was true for a girl who dreamed a man with a pistol shot her in the cheek. She woke up to find a large pimple had just erupted in the exact spot where the dream wound had been. She was emotionally distressed – and she had a big "zit" too!

Your dreaming mind can pick up small changes in your physical body and magnify them into vivid pictures. If you dream you are wounded in a certain area of your body, and you can feel the pain in the dream, be sure that there is not something physical that needs attention or treatment in that spot.

Beastly Parents

Many kids have dreams about a parent who is an animal or becomes one. One girl had a terrifying dream that her mother is standing at her bedroom door; she smiles, revealing vampire fangs. Another dreamed her mother turns into a black octopus blocking the door to prevent her leaving; Mom strikes her with one of her eight arms. Still another dreamed that her mother and her aunt (who lived with them) look normal, but she can see that under their dresses and masks they are wolves preparing to attack her.

Fear of a parent's anger is understandable. Parents try to impose standards of behavior on their kids. Sometimes they are unreasonable or unfair, and turn into beasts in their child's dreams. As you find your way from being a dependent child to becoming an adult responsible for your own behavior, such dreams are normal.

In some dreams, it's the dreamer who's the wild beast. A man told me how much he suffered as a kid from nightmares about becoming a werewolf. He didn't know anything about the natural body changes that happen during puberty. When he noticed dark hair starting to grow on his arms and chest, he began to dream he was turning into a werewolf. It was not until he got some good counseling that he understood the natural processes going on in his body.

The Supernatural Dream Villain

You may be one of those dreamers who struggle to escape a supernatural creature. These are not realistic people or animals, but beings from other realms – legends, fantasies, television, movies, folk or fairy tales. It is the sense of evil or the dread you feel about a supernatural enemy that is important. Kids dream of supernatural attackers at about the same rate (16 percent) as adults.

Here are some supernatural or imaginary beings that appear in kids' dreams:

- Monsters and demons are after me.
- The Devil is chasing me.
- Weird creatures are trying to catch me.
- I'm caught by vampires.
- Zombies are following me.
- The Chinese form of death gets me.
- Elves and witches are trying to trap me.

Vampires in dreams may suggest more than fear of the supernatural or that you recently saw a horror movie. Vampires, like werewolves, can be a sign of transformation. If you dream about a vampire being after you, trying to suck blood or change you into a vampire, the explanation can be as simple as feeling your body entering adolescence. You are becoming an adult. It means your body and your thinking will undergo a change.

The Evil Force and Fear of Death

A man told me the alarming childhood dreams he had after the death of his father. He had last seen his severely ill dad carried from the house on a stretcher, across the entryway, beyond an outside grilled door, and into a waiting ambulance. He never saw his father alive again. Soon he began to have this dream: He is coming home from school carrying his red and green plaid schoolbag. He presses the buzzer on the outer grilled door. After he is let in, he crosses the area between the outer and inner door where he had last seen his father alive. There he hears the cellar door, connecting to the entryway, open. He hurries up the steps to his front door, hearing the tread of heavy footsteps closing in behind. He cannot see who is after him but knows it's getting close.

He always awoke from this dream in a panic. His fear was most likely that of death: the unknown unseen force that had snatched his father away right at the spot the dream took place. The space between the inner and outer world, between the street and the front door, symbolized the separation between life and death. Night after night he confronted it alone in his dreams. Once he grew up, he said the experience of his father's death and the nightmares that followed it was the tragedy of his life from which he never fully recovered. Nothing could change the fact that his father had died, but he needed help to deal with the recurrent nightmare.

Although this dreamer's experience was extreme, a vague evil "thing" is the enemy in both kids' and adults' dreams about 10 percent of the time. Many kids dream about something closing in on them that is unseen and unknown:

- I'm chased by something I can't see but I know it's evil.
- I can't see the thing that's after me but I can hear it calling threats.
- I'm chased by something surrounded by black energy.

If you find yourself pursued by something you know is evil but you can't quite make it out, you are probably anxious about something you are not yet ready to face directly. When you have this kind of dream enemy, you'll need to be patient until you feel stronger. Some of the suggestions later in this chapter may be helpful.

The Bad Guys and Girls You Know

Some nightmares make it very clear who the dream villains are. Only 7 percent of kids' dreams include a dream villain they know:

- My twin brother tries to poison me.
- A man I like tries to kill me with a sword.
- My former best friend's mother tries to hit me with a frying pan.
- A friend of the family chases me.
- A boy from school attempts to stab me.
- My mother in the clothing of a devil tries to murder me.

Think back to the dreams in which the mother turned into a threatening vampire, a black octopus, and a wolf. In such dreams, people close to us either make us uncomfortable, or people we like have recently behaved in a way that felt scary to us.

Seventeen-year-old Shauna dreamed that Kurt Cobain from the grunge rock group Nirvana chased her with a knife. She needed to ask herself questions about what Kurt Cobain meant to her. Whenever you don't know your dream enemy personally, ask yourself these questions:

1. What is special or unique about this person?
2. Who or what does he or she remind me of?

Your answers will help you understand the meaning of your dream. For instance, if you think of Kurt Cobain as an exciting musician who was cute and sexy, you probably want someone this attractive in your romantic life. If you think of Kurt Cobain as a dangerous figure who dabbled in drugs and died, you may be warning yourself that something you are doing is risky.

Ask yourself these same questions about other characters in your dreams, including ones you know. When you dream about your grandmother, for example, you may not be dreaming about the actual person, but about some quality she represents to you. The meaning depends on your answers to the questions. Your grandmother might have an old-fashioned way of doing things; she might stand for overly strict discipline, or she could have an especially warm loving quality.

Odd Objects

Sometimes the thing chasing you in a dream is completely weird, as in the case of the twelve-year-old girl who said, "I was fleeing from a giant napkin." Although this kind of dream is pretty rare, other kids have been chased in their dreams by odd objects:

- A bubble is chasing me through town.
- A large rolling orange is coming after me.
- A car with no one in it speeds behind me.

Each bizarre object makes sense in the dreamer's life. A woman who had recurrent dreams about being chased by a gooey egg had been force-fed as a child. A child who was chased by a tortilla felt hounded by her mother, who made tortillas. A man who was chased by a giant dust ball was obsessed with cleanliness. A student who dreamed of being chased in and out of buses and all over town by a large white paper was having trouble with a college report.

If you dream about a weird attacker, you'll have to do some dream detective work. Ask yourself, "What does this odd object make me think of? Do I associate it with any person or thing in my waking life?" Answers to these questions will give you clues to the meaning of odd villains in your dreams.

Portrait of a Dream Villain

You can get additional clues to understanding what your dream means by thinking about the main characteristics of your dream enemy. The qualities often mentioned by dreamers are color; size; hair and skin; weapons; and teeth, beaks, claws, or horns.

The final meaning of any dream image depends on your personal associations to it. However, many images have similar meanings to many dreamers. Here is a list that might help you think in the right direction. But remember that *your* answers to what these qualities suggest to you is the most important.

Color Many kids describe the thing, animal, or person after them as being dressed in black. Or the awful thing in pursuit may be "surrounded by black energy." Just as the villain in cowboy movies wears a black hat, the bad guys in our dreams often wear dark clothing. In nightmares, black usually suggests danger; in good dreams, it suggests mystery or power.

Size Most kids describe the dream enemy as being gigantic. Large size usually stands for the dreamer's sense of feeling overwhelmed by fear. In positive dreams, this quality can indicate awesome importance. When your dream enemies are small, they tend to be either poisonous (such as spiders, wasps, or snakes) or multiple (like a swarm of bees, hundreds of rats, thousands of bugs). If the tiny dream enemies are venomous, you might feel infected by an emotional hurt from something that happened in waking life. If they are multiple, you feel overwhelmed by many troublesome elements that "bug" or besiege you.

Hair and Skin Dreamers often mention the hair of their assailant. It may be described as wild or chaotic, which usually suggests crazy confused thinking. It may be white or silver, which is sometimes associated with aging or with evil wizardry in the dreamer's mind; in good dreams, white or silver hair indicates a wise person. If your dream enemy is bearded, it may suggest evil danger; in good dreams, it may imply wisdom. If your attacker is bald, he may be the dangerous strength you sense in someone in waking life; in good dreams, baldness can mean supportive strength. Scarred skin in a dream enemy suggests danger of a primitive or savage kind; in good dreams, it may stand for a healing initiation.

Weapons Weapons are extensions of the human body. Knives and swords are more effective forms of nails or claws; they lengthen the reach of the human arm. Guns are more powerful forms of punching fists; they sometimes represent a sexual threat from a man. People who have suffered actual attacks in waking life, with or without weapons, are often tormented by nightmares replaying the attack. It's important for such dreamers to get counseling.

Natural Defenses Claws or talons on your dream enemy suggest you feel like a victim to cutting wounding actions or words while awake; in good dreams, these may protect you. Horns or antlers on your dream enemy suggest that sharp penetrating speech or actions are directed toward you in anger; in positive dreams, extensions from the head suggest expansive ideas.

Cutting to the Chase

What would this big bad creature, person, or thing in your dream do to you if it could catch you? For children, the answer is often "eat me." For some children, as well as for most older kids or adults, the reply is "hurt me or kill me."

If you have dreams of being chased or attacked, there is something you can do. When you are awake, practice the steps below. Simply imagining a better outcome to a scary dream can give future dreams a better outcome. We are especially suggestible during the drowsy periods before and after sleep – visualizing positive dream scenes is best at these times.

Turn around and face the dream enemy. Simply confronting the thing that is chasing you in a dream is sometimes enough to disarm it. At times, tigers turn into kittens.

If it continues to threaten you, get help. Because it's your dream, you can call for help, but deal with it by yourself until assistance arrives. Remember that you can summon special weapons or powers.

Ask it, "Who are you? What do you want?" You may be surprised by the answers that you get. I once turned to a dream dog that was nipping at my heels and challenged it by asking, "Why are you doing that?" It said, "Because I want your attention." Sometimes dream attackers want love!

Offer to make friends with it if it will help you. Surprisingly, dream figures sometimes give us gifts in exchange for changes in our behavior.

If the dream figure has become friendlier, you can try to slip inside it. Sometimes we can learn something important by imagining ourselves inside the figure. Is there some quality in this figure you could benefit from making part of yourself? More confidence? More strength? You can sample this in your imagination.

Do something fun with the former dream enemy. If you wish, you can play with the figure by being happy with it, by dancing, swimming, or flying with it. One girl took a joyful ride on the back of the fish that had been threatening her.

Accept the dream figure. Some dreamers like to picture the former dream enemy surrounded with golden light. They open their hearts to it and love it despite all.

You might reach a point where you can use these suggestions while you are still inside your dream! You have far more power in your dreams than you realize. It's your dream. You can use it to understand yourself. You can let its images teach you. You can tap into the magic stored in your dream.

2

Kisses Are Delicious

"One of my friends is in love, and she has a good banana. I peel mine. Inside it is rotten and has a brown tube running through it, so I throw it away. A bunch of kids go to order banana splits with cherry sauce and whipped cream. I don't think I get one."

– Patti, 16

Love is one of life's main delights. Perhaps that's why being in love, yearning for love, and being loved appear in dreams as another of life's pleasures – delicious food. When you dream of sipping the most divine drink that ever passed your lips, or savoring the sweet hot fudge sauce and cool smooth ice cream of a yummy banana split, you're not just sampling dream food. You're sampling the idea of boyfriends and girlfriends.

There might be a physical reason why dream images of food and drink symbolize kisses. An expert in animal behavior believes that kissing is nature's way of having partners exchange an addictive substance that chemically forms emotional bonds between them. The chemicals in each person's sebum – the fatty substance from tiny glands on the face, scalp, neck, and sexual parts of the body – are transferred in the sucking action of kissing, since there is a lot of sebum on the inside of the lips. Eagles and other birds bond this way when they trade food gifts in mating. Perhaps people get "addicted" to the taste of their partner.

The connection between food images in dreams and love might also come from the nursing of newborns. Being cuddled in loving arms while being fed makes a powerful link between food and love in the minds of babies.

Food and Love

You'll dream about food when you're just plain hungry. Eight-year-old Shalina dreamed of sweets: "I am going to school and on my way I see trees laden with toffees and candies." Lots of kids dream about pizza and picnic snacks. Explorers who were deprived of food to the point of starvation reported dreaming of great feasts. A hiker who was lost in the Sierra Mountains for several weeks after breaking an ankle – surviving on ants, moss, and water – dreamed he was avidly eating steaks and fish. Even when we've only skipped dinner, we're still likely to dream of eating.

We also dream about food when we're hungry for love. The seven-year-old girl who told me she dreamed "My sister had a birthday and I was mad because my mom would not give me any cake" was hungry for more than cake. She wanted to be fed with her mother's love that she felt was going to her sister.

What are the foods you associate with feeling loved and nurtured?

❈

To dream of eating delicious food is to want emotional nourishment.

❈

What's Your Favorite Treat?

People of all ages make their desires for love into dream images. A woman who was unhappy in her marriage had a favorite dream of a beautiful place with a field, forest, and stream between her and a patch of wild strawberries. An electric fence separates her from this "forbidden fruit." She finds the way around the fence, crossing over the stream to gather the ripe morsels. She felt this dream was a vision of a happy romantic relationship that she could have if she dared.

A sixteen-year-old girl had a similar dream of eating forbidden fruit, squeezing the goodness from it, but she felt it was wrong and that she should wait to taste such pleasures.

Patti (whose dream starts this chapter) had this dream about food when she was fourteen: "At school in the cafeteria, I'm waiting in line for soup. When I get near the pot of orange-colored soup that bubbles up and down, the popular girl in my class jumps into it. Then a snake rises out of the pot. A boy in the class puts his hand around the snake that instantly turns into cans of vegetables and fruits." To Patti's dreaming mind, the popular girl had become part of the food for boys. She watched with interest, but didn't join the other girl in the pot. Patti was never deprived of food, so both these dreams probably symbolize the yummy things she imagined would be hers when she was properly loved.

Sexual parts of the body often appear in dreams as plump ripe fruit. In dreams, drinks and other fluids might be hinting at sex, too. If such foods or drinks appear in your dreams when you are not hungry or thirsty, you may be dreaming about romance. Notice what your attitude is toward them in the dream: are you disgusted, or do you find the dream food or drink divine? This can tell you a lot about whether or not you feel ready to make sex a part of your life.

Hugs and Kisses

The sweetness of a kiss, the warmth of a hug, the joy of a wedding day – everyone's happiest dreams are sometimes about these things.

Girls begin to dream about getting married when they are quite young. They dream a lot about wedding gowns. A seven-year-old girl dreamed about her doll (symbolizing herself) getting married. An eight-year-old girl dreamed that a boy she liked married someone else, got divorced, and then married her.

Boys, too, sometimes dream of weddings to come. Ten-year-old Asgar dreamed about the wedding of his teacher (a man he admired), with the groom wearing a garland around his neck. The house was full of flowers, lit candles, cheer, and good food for all.

Dream Feasts

As you get older, the huge hormonal shifts in your body can lead to unbroken sleep marathons. Remember: the more you sleep, the more you dream. These hormonal changes also make you more aware of your body. No wonder kids dream so much about love. You probably do, too.

This tendency for kids to dream about love is encouraged by rituals in many cultures. Several folk traditions supposedly make you dream about your future lover. In France, girls chant a rhyme to the full moon in spring; they are told to back into bed while keeping their eyes focused on the moon, in order to sleep and dream about the boyfriends in their future. In Romania, girls let their hair down at midnight in spring, gaze at the full moon, and wish to see the face of "the one I will love forever." In bed, they place their own rings under the pillow to help bring on a dream of their true love. This tradition survives in the practice of taking home a piece of wedding cake to put under your pillow to bring dreams of your future sweetheart. You might get a similar effect with photos of your favorite rock star plastered on your bedroom wall or perched on your dresser.

In her diary, thirteen-year-old Anne Frank recorded her romantic longings for Peter, the young man who shared the hidden attic with her family in Amsterdam during World War II. She said she fell asleep seeing his image and continued to see him in her dreams. When she was awake, she wondered if she could keep her longing for him under control. These same longings appear in the dreams of kids today:

- There's a girl I really like more than other people and I meet her in a dream, hug her and kiss her. In "real" life I never kiss her on the mouth.
- In a recent dream I end up finding an old friend I loved in high school . . . We go walking down these streets in an area I don't ever go to, but I know the area. I end up seeing this chick in

her doorway so I run over to meet her. Well this leads to
hugging, then talking.
• I am with someone I love.

When you dream about the pleasures of hugging and kissing, you
may have mixed feelings, as many kids do. In fact, a number of kids
have bad dreams about boyfriends or girlfriends cheating on them.
These dreams are usually based on the dreamer's feeling of insecurity.

If you're dreaming happily about the love in your life, relish it. Hugs
and kisses, and luscious food that symbolizes the delicious exchange of
loving feelings, are dreams to be savored.

3

Hanging Out with the Famous

"Ewan McGregor is in my dream, looking so cute! His soft voice and accent are very clear. I am madly in love with him and want to introduce him to a girl who is with me for some reason. I ask him to draw or sign some pictures but he puts me off. I want it done now. He gets angry and refuses. He seems to regard me as a little girl, but I keep on adoring him just the same."

– Megan, 13

Megan is yearning to be a grown-up woman, one who would inspire the devoted love of someone as attractive as Ewan McGregor seems to her. But her dream suggests that she's not ready for that stage of life.

Most kids dream about famous people they wish they could be with, ones who would bring glamour or fame into their lives, ones who would love them the way they want. You've probably had some of these dreams yourself.

❋

To dream of happily being with a celebrity
is to wish for a quality that person possesses.

❋

For many dreamers, the celebrity is often a figure from popular culture. Children mostly dream about people from television shows, movies, and stories.

Boys often dream about famous sports figures, or teams they would like to know or join. One dreamed of playing in a championship basketball game against the Chicago Bulls – in his dream, he plays against Michael Jordan and beats him. This suggests a wish for the lifestyle, money, and attention Michael Jordan represents to the dreamer. It is the dreamer's own ambitions taking shape.

Teenage girls are more likely to dream about being in love with a movie, TV, or music star. One girl dreamed of being on a tour with the Backstreet Boys; her favorite Backstreet Boy falls in love with and marries her. Other girls dream about being Buffy the Vampire Slayer. These dreams express a longing for the love, admiration, and power the dreamer thinks the celebrity possesses.

Whoever your favorite musical star, sports figure, or television celebrity might be, this person is the one most likely to make an appearance in your dreams. Movies or TV shows you watch just before you sleep also influence your dreams that follow.

Celebrity Detection

What famous person would you like to be? Why? Who would you choose for a dream lover? What's their special appeal for you?

You may need to do a little dream detective work to pinpoint why you've selected a particular person. Sixteen-year-old Kate was having dreams about actress Julia Stiles. She began to ask herself why she was dreaming about this popular blonde actress – what was her unique or special quality? Julia Stiles came from the same town, New York, where Kate grew up. In the TV miniseries *The '60s*, Julia Stiles played a character named Katie; in the movie *Ten Things I Hate About You*, she played a character called Kat. Kate's dreams seemed to say that, if a girl from New York could grow up to be a famous movie star playing strong characters with Kate's name, there was hope for her. When we have good dreams about a celebrity, there's always a reason. We identify with something about them. They represent a part of ourselves and what we want in life.

If you dream about a celebrity, consider these things:

1. Who is the famous person in your dream? Describe the kind of person he or she is.
2. Name three outstanding traits of this star. What is unique?
3. Are these qualities you want more of in your life?
4. Is there any special significance in the person's name?
5. Does this celebrity's name or appearance resemble someone you know?

Whether your dream about a celebrity is a good one or a nightmare, it's helpful to know what the famous person means to you, so you're better equipped to understand its meaning.

The Love Connection

Some kids dream about making passionate love with a star. Anyone who is seen to be powerful may play the role of dream lover, from the president of a country to the latest heartthrob on TV. Actors from TV series star in romantic dreams, as do famous rock singers and movie actors. Your dreams of this type can even provide "practice" for future real-life loves.

Other teens have nightmares involving celebrities. "I was raped by the killer from the movie *Scream*," said eighteen-year-old Brittany. And remember Shauna, who dreamed about being chased by the rock star Kurt Cobain with a knife?

These dreams suggest that the dreamers are afraid they or someone close to them has some of the same qualities the famous person has. A generation of children were frightened by the wicked witch in the movie *The Wizard of Oz*. The bad guys from the *Star Wars* movies appear in nightmares: Darth Vader in his black helmet, armor, and cape; Darth Maul with his mysterious face paint. In these movies and in horror films, the characters onscreen seem to resemble people you know in their meanest mood: the mother who gets furious; the father who is overly harsh; the boyfriend who is too possessive or too rough; the girlfriend who betrays you.

Always try to see behind the image of the star in your dreams to the face of the person or the quality that they represent.

Power Connections

Boys often dream about Superman, while some girls dream about Wonder Woman or a good witch. These imaginary characters express the dreamers' wishes to be stronger, with more power over their lives. Kids who dream of superheroes also want the protection such figures provide. One young boy dreamed "I was killed in a space adventure but Han Solo brought me back to life." Five-year-old Aidan dreamed that Dracula and ghosts were trying to suck his blood but Casper the Friendly Ghost wouldn't let them do it.

In the same way, kids and adults dream about sports figures, political leaders, royalty, and other important people who are able to make an impact on the world, who have power that is unavailable to most of us.

Artistic Connections

Some dreamers yearn for a connection with a famous person who has a talent or ability they wish for themselves. Is there a fantastic singer in your dream? An amazing pianist? An artist you admire? A great writer? You may be yearning to connect with the abilities these people have. You could be preparing to develop your own talents in the same direction.

Punny Connections

When you dream about a famous person, always pay particular attention to his or her name, in case your dreaming mind is creating a pun. A woman dreamed about being kissed by the comedian Bob Hope, who she was not at all attracted to. However, the dreamer was feeling discouraged about a project. To be "kissed by *hope*" was the very thing that she wanted.

If someone in your dream has a name like "Art" or "Newman," think about whether there is a pun involved for you. Are you wanting to have more *art* activities in your free time? Is there a *new man* in your life? You'll be surprised how often puns pop up in your dreams once you begin to look for them.

Connections All Your Own

Some people dream about a famous person who represents a spiritual connection to them. One woman dreamed of a friend named Faith in her spiritual dreams.

You need to explore each famous person who makes an appearance in your dream, since you will see a star very differently from the way someone else sees the same figure.

A British journalist had a dream of having tea with Queen Elizabeth. In it, she played the violin for him. For this man, Queen Elizabeth represented "ultimate good taste," while violin music had "great emotional warmth." This was the combination – good taste and emotional warmth – he desired in his writing. But if you dream about a royal person, you might be focusing on the power and authority they have instead. In order to get your personal meaning, it's important to give your own descriptions of the celebrity who appears in your dream.

When you dream about a famous person, you have a chance to learn more about yourself, to understand what is attractive to you and what you dislike at this time. Remember that your tastes will change. The stars' lives change, too, so that what a particular celebrity means to you today might be quite different from what that same star will represent a few years from now. As you get to know the stars in your dreams, you'll be getting to know yourself at a deeper level. You'll be exploring your inner life in ways that will lead to self-discovery. You'll be ready for new adventures in your waking space.

4

Ow! My Teeth Are Crumbling

"I become aware that something's wrong with my teeth. They're cracking apart in my mouth. I spit bloody pieces out into my hand. One tooth dangles loose, hanging from a fiber. I wake up feeling weird and check to feel if my teeth are still there."

— Molly, 14

You'll probably wake up puzzled if you have the dream that your teeth are crumbling. People are often surprised by this common nightmare. What could cause this bizarre dream, which is remarkably consistent from dreamer to dreamer? There is scarcely a mention of it in any book. Some experts think it suggests a fear of old age. If this were true, the dream would be more frequent among older adults, yet people of all ages have this nightmare. Most are bewildered by it.

Over my years of dream collecting and study I think I've found the explanation. When one dreamer told me that she actually chipped a bit off a tooth during this dream and found it in her mouth when she awoke, it seemed like my suspicions were confirmed.

I think there are two factors involved in dreams about teeth crumbling apart. The first is physical, the second psychological.

Grinding Teeth

Many people clench their jaws and/or grind their teeth during sleep. Dentists call this behavior "bruxism." It is sometimes so severe that people have to sleep wearing a bite plate, a dental device to prevent tooth grinding. Experts estimate that one in seven people gnash their teeth during sleep. When people grind their teeth every night over a long period of time, it results in permanent damage to the teeth.

If you happen to grit your teeth or clench your jaws during sleep, you will create a sensation in your mouth of pressure, even discomfort. This sensation will be picked up by the dreaming mind, and the physical pressure in your mouth will prompt a dream.

The Clenched Jaw of Anger

If you've never been told you grind your teeth, the dream might be caused by a psychological factor. Almost anytime you are angry, the muscles in your jaw automatically tighten. You clench your jaw to control an outburst of angry words. You hold in angry feelings because it may not be appropriate to express them, or you will be criticized or punished for doing so.

Our teeth, like those of other mammals, are sometimes used as a means of defense. We may feel an urge to use them when we are in hostile situations.

As you relax into sleep after a day in which you felt angry but did not voice it, or said harsh things anyway and still feel angry, your intense emotions have not vanished. During sleep these feelings often surface, resulting in you gritting your teeth or clenching your jaw. Your dreaming mind picks up the physical expression of anger in your mouth and the emotional feelings of anger you've held back. You dream that your teeth are coming apart.

❋

To dream that your teeth are crumbling is
to feel resentful about some waking-life event.

❋

Take the Bite out of Bad Dreams

If you dream that your teeth are falling out, get them checked. If you suspect that you grind your teeth at night, you'll want to discuss the situation with your dentist.

Whether the cause of your dream is physical, emotional, or both, it's wise to find ways to relax your jaw. It's important to explore any feelings of anger or resentment you have. Are you feeling defenseless? Are you unable to say what you need to say? Do you want to talk back to some person in authority? Tell off the class bully? Say what you really think to someone who annoys you?

Find safe places to express your true feelings. Practice saying what you want to say. Talk about your feelings to helpful people. Work through your anger, let it go, or guide it into positive creative paths while you are awake. One woman wrote a poem based on her dream about tooth trouble: "Gum stuck in mouth, trapped in places not wanted, words left unsaid." The simple act of putting her thoughts onto paper defused their power to disturb her. Give it a try, and you may start smiling in your dreams.

5

Weirdo at the Wheel

.

"I'm in a car with a crazy woman at the steering wheel. We're going too fast and about to crash. I am trying to get the wheel from her."

– Caroline, 14

When Caroline was fourteen, her family moved to another country. She and her mother traveled ahead of her father, who was to arrive two weeks later. Caroline and her mother were staying in a hotel, while they looked for a place to live. When she told her mother about her dream, it was obvious that Caroline's dream mind saw her mother as the "crazy driver" who had taken her from her familiar space to a foreign country, where she felt life was totally out of her control.

Kids around the world share the same struggle – to take control of their own lives. They still need parents for protection, for money, food, shelter, and family interaction. At the same time, they want to do what they want to do, make their own decisions, choose their own friends, and more. It's a constant tug-of-war over the steering wheel of life.

Your dreams probably picture some version of your effort to be in charge of your own fate. You might be in the passenger seat or the backseat when you realize there's no one at the steering wheel; or some totally unreliable person is driving, so you desperately try to gain control. You might be struggling to manage a truck, trying to start a boat motor, or at the control panel of an airplane that's having problems – you might not even know how to operate the thing. Many kids dream about being in an out-of-control vehicle long before they know how to drive or have their own driver's license. So do children who are much too young to drive and adults who have never driven. If you have this common nightmare, you'll probably wake up feeling alarmed.

✳

To dream of being in a car in trouble is to
feel you've lost control in a waking situation.

✳

In one study, 30 percent of 100 kids reported having a dream about trouble driving a vehicle; adults reported it more often (38 percent), perhaps because driving is so much a part of their lives.

When you dream of a problem driving a car, it's likely to take one of these forms:

• Your brakes don't work or you've lost control for some other reason.

- Someone else is in the driver's seat.
- The road conditions are poor.
- Your car is damaged.

Each has something different to tell you about yourself and your feelings.

I Have No Brakes!

If you dream you have no brakes, or poor ones, it suggests that you are moving too fast for good control right now. Are you trying to accomplish too much in too little time? Are you pushing too hard in school or sports or to finish a project? Your dream is a warning to slow down so you don't "crash" by becoming sick or having an accident. Look at your waking life – be careful.

If you dream that your steering wheel comes off or won't respond, you're having difficulty getting where you want to go in waking life. A boy dreamed the handlebars of his bicycle came off; a girl couldn't make the steering wheel of a car turn. Such dreams suggest that the dreamer feels unable to direct things. Think about how you are trying to handle things in waking life so that you can take charge of achieving your goals.

If you dream that your car is going the wrong direction, rolling downhill when you want to go upward, or backward when you want to go forward, you're not moving through waking life the way you want to go right now. Missing a turn suggests you've passed by something you want. Taking a wrong turn can mean you've gone astray. Being at a crossroads symbolizes making life choices. Reaching a dead end suggests you've made a wrong choice. When you wake up, you should reexamine your plans, rethink what you want and ways to reach your target.

My Car Won't Go

Some problems with dream cars arise because there isn't enough power. Instead of going too fast, the car goes too slow or won't move. One woman dreamed she was parked on the wrong side of the road when she was struck head-on by a truck; another dreamed her car was stuck in idle; yet another that her car reverted to a "Flintstones" car that she had to "run" by foot power. A boy dreamed he jumped into a boat but was unable to get the motor started no matter how hard he tried; he had to slowly paddle by hand. Other variations of this dream problem include dead batteries and running low or out of gas.

Such dreams almost always indicate a lack of physical force and a low energy level. If you have a dream about this type of car trouble, you can be fairly sure that your energy level or interest in some waking project is running low. Sometimes this dream occurs when the dreamer has a health problem that creates reduced energy. If you suspect this, talk to your family doctor. If you think your dream is caused by lack of interest, think about your activities and decide whether you want to choose a different way.

I'm Not in Control of the Car

When you are not at the steering wheel of your dream car, you feel some other person or part of yourself is directing your life at the moment. One girl dreamed that, while her friend was driving the car, the driver took her hands off the wheel and swerved into a store, while the dreamer desperately tried to grab the wheel and regain control. A woman dreamed a three-year-old child was driving – the toddler stands for the spoiled child part of herself. A little girl dreamed a witch, representing the girl's angry mother, was driving her car.

If you dream someone else is in control of your dream car, describe that person in a phrase or a brief sentence. Whatever you say is likely to be the aspect of yourself or someone else that you feel is in charge of your life currently. You need to change things to feel more in control.

I Can't Drive

Several children and older kids dream they are forced to drive but they don't know how: one girl said, "I am in a car with my sister and have to bring her somewhere quickly but I don't know how to drive." If you have this dream, ask yourself if there is something you feel pushed to do or take charge of that is beyond your abilities at this time.

Sometimes the driver in the dream knows how to drive but is unable to do so:

• I am paralyzed while trying to drive a car.

If you dream this version, think about what's preventing you from operating in the way you wish in the waking world.

One girl dreamed that no one is at the wheel of her car: she jumps into the driver's seat, but finds her feet can't reach the pedals, and she can't turn the wheel. When no one is driving your dream car, you probably feel that your life is out of your control at the moment. Driving your own dream car suggests that you are in better control of your waking world.

Road Conditions Are Dangerous

When you dream of car trouble, the dream setting is probably a risky place, such as a bad area of the city at night. You may be driving in the woods, or down an unlit country lane with no guideposts.

Many car trouble dreams are set near the edge of a cliff: "I drive off the road, because it ends around a corner on the face of a cliff." Lots of dreamers go over a cliff in a car. Such dreams suggest that the dreamers feel at the brink of a risky situation in waking life. If you have this dream, remember that you have the power to steer the car to a safe landing. Just because a dangerous drop-off is nearby, you do not have to go over it.

At times dreamers travel roads slick with rain or rutted with mud, with their vision obscured by heavy rain, snow, ice, or fog. Some dream drivers drive up or down mountains on twisty narrow roads. The hazardous paths in these dreams express the difficult conditions dreamers are traveling through in the waking environment. Such dreams remind you to be careful – you're on dangerous turf. Go slow. Take care.

Your Dream Car

Many kids dream that their cars get damaged:

- Before I got my license I dreamed I was forced to drive but I didn't know how so I crashed into the garage.
- No matter how hard I try to steer away from the wall, I scratch the side of the car.
- I'm driving a car and lose control and it flips over.

Like houses, cars in dreams often represent the dreamer's body or current lifestyle. Like dream wounds (see chapter 1 "Oh No, It's After Me!"), damage to your dream car can refer to an actual physical problem or an emotional hurt, and sometimes both. Old or injured people often picture their dream cars having problems that stand for their physical limitations, as one older man did when he dreamed his favorite car was in a used-car lot, run-down with cracked windows. Another man, who lost his temper during the daytime, dreamed that night that the radiator in his car overheated, and the cap blew off; his dream was picturing his angry "blow up."

Many kids have strong opinions about different types and brands of cars. The same kind of car will be hated by one dreamer and adored by another. If your dream is about a particular style or brand or size of car, describe how you feel about it. This will give you an important clue to the meaning of your dream.

People who have been injured and are beginning to heal often dream about driving great cars with "good handling ability" and "excellent brakes." People who gain weight and pregnant women often dream of driving large bulky vehicles, such as trucks or buses. One pregnant woman dreamed she was driving with the spare tire around her midsection, an image of her expanding waistline. When people feel good about their bodies and how they're moving through life at the moment, they sometimes dream about classic cars with powerful engines.

Consider the cars and other vehicles that appear in your dreams. Ask yourself:

1. How is this car or model or brand different from others similar to it?
2. What's special about the car in my dream?

See what your dream cars have to tell you about how you feel about yourself right now.

Other Dream Vehicles

Your dream might involve a bicycle, a truck, a train, or some other vehicle that moves on land. You might be at the helm of a ship, a motor-boat, or some other vehicle that goes through water. You might dream of flying an airplane, a helicopter, a spaceship, or another vehicle that moves through air. Dream problems can have added complications, depending on the element these vehicles move through. Underground in a subway there is the danger of collapse; sailing over water risks storms and drowning; moving through air has the added possibility of crashing from a great height.

Although each type of vehicle has its unique aspects, the major problems you will encounter in dreams about them are the same that arise in dreams about car trouble. You should ask yourself the same questions:

1. How much control do I have?
2. Am I able to speed up and slow down at will?
3. Can I go in the direction I wish?
4. Do conditions permit me to travel?
5. Can I avoid sustaining damage while moving where and how I want to go?

Road-Mapping Your Dream Life

Most of the problems you will dream about with cars or other vehicles involve wild and reckless movement or too little power and control. As you develop your ability to choose your path in life, you will be able to drive your dream cars with increasing skill. You will decide which direction to go and how fast.

Remember – you have the ability to prevent yourself going over the edge of a cliff, and also of moving through space by choice. You can steer yourself upward and land safely. You can select which dream road to follow to adventure. You can drive your own dream car comfortably or allow a reliable person to drive for you. You can move over smooth roads under clear skies. You dream cars can be in top condition, looking good and responding to your needs. You can drive the model, brand, and size of car you desire on the highways of your dreams. Sometimes you may travel into other spatial dimensions, using a giant steering wheel or riding through the skies on a magic dream carpet.

As your skills in dream driving increase, you will be expressing your growing power to affect your waking destiny. Positive aspects of your self will be in charge, and you'll feel more satisfied with the "driving" conditions in your life. You'll be more able to cope, to solve problems, and to steer yourself along life's journey.

6

I Forgot to Study for the Test

"The teacher gives me a long list of questions from a French book that I didn't read . . ."

— Karel, 15

If you dream of having to take a test for which you are completely unprepared, or forgetting your lines when you're performing in a play onstage, you'll probably feel anxious during the dream and puzzled when you wake up. Especially if you do not have a big test or performance scheduled, you'll wonder why you dreamed about one.

This nightmare has many variations. You may not know the answers to the questions in a test; you may have read the wrong books or studied for the wrong exam. Maybe you intended to drop the course, didn't know that you were registered for it, or simply forgot to study. You may not have enough time to write down the answers. For some dreamers, the difficulty is getting to where the test is taking place, running down hallways, searching for the right room. You may not even make it to the school building: thirteen-year-old Bronwen said, "I wake up late and no matter how hard I try to get there on time, I can't get to the test."

In another version of this bad dream, you flub a performance onstage. In dramas, musicals, sports, or some other event, you realize you've forgotten the lines, don't know the part, are missing vital equipment, or don't know what to do:

- I forget the words of the song.
- I am in a gymnastics competition and I fall on each element.
- I'm onstage, making it up as I go along.

Your dreams of performing poorly can help you understand how you are feeling at the moment. They alert you so that you can change your behavior and be more prepared.

Dreams of Poor Performance

Performing poorly in school or onstage is a fairly common nightmare among teenagers. More than one-quarter of kids who were surveyed said they'd had these dreams. Surprisingly, more adults (40 percent) report this dream than kids in school do. One man said, "I'm taking my law exam and am afraid I'll fail. It's ridiculous because I graduated long ago and have been a practicing lawyer for more than twenty years." Doctors, lawyers, engineers, and other professionals have these dreams long after finishing graduate training. So, if you don't dream of poor performance now, you may when you are older.

Why do people who have been free of the tensions of taking exams for many years put themselves through the discomfort of doing so in a dream? The answer is simple: people feel their performance in their jobs or in some other area of their waking world may not be adequate.

❋

To dream of performing poorly in a test or onstage is to feel unprepared in a waking situation.

❋

Testing – One, Two, Three

Generally, when you dream about doing badly on a school test, you are feeling unprepared to cope with some waking situation and you fear you might fail. If you dream you are taking an exam or participating in a performance, you are confronting a challenge in your current life. You face a new or unexpected life test. You're not sure how to handle it. You feel confused, or think you don't have enough time to do well.

When you dream that you "forget" you have a test, and you actually have one in your waking life, your dream is a strong reminder to get to work. A boy dreamed "I forgot to study for a history test"; if he had one on that subject coming up, he needed to start studying right away.

More often, the nightmare of doing poorly on a test is symbolic. You might know the feeling of not knowing the answers on a test or of not having read the material. When you find yourself facing some other life situation that you feel unprepared for, you have the same feelings as when you were struggling to pass a test in school. You're feeling judged on your performance.

Do you have a date with someone you really want to impress? Are you going for your first part-time job interview? Are you trying out for a special program or club? Are you worried you might not be good enough at kissing and all that? Any number of situations put kids in the position of being evaluated too early. You are facing a lot of firsts, and each one can seem like the ultimate test. Be comfortable. Soon you'll be through with these challenges. You'll be more experienced and feel more confident about coping with future ones.

Playing a Part

When you dream about being in the wrong play or doing poorly in an onstage performance, you may sense that you are "playing the wrong part" or don't know your role in some waking-life situation.

Many famous and successful people are troubled by dreams about performing poorly. The celebrated photographer Ansel Adams, who originally trained as a classical pianist, was troubled by dreams of poor performance. In his recurring dream, he is scheduled to play, gets onstage to do so, and has the awful realization that he doesn't know the piece of music. Actor Sean Penn, while filming the role of a jazz guitarist in Woody Allen's movie *Sweet and Lowdown*, said he had nightmares that he is trying to play a guitar solo but his fingers "can't find the strings." These dreams are typical of feeling unprepared for a waking-life challenge.

Fifteen-year-old Tara plays clarinet, and she often dreams that she's trying to but can't, as if she's forgotten how. In her dreams, the bandleader scolds her. Tara probably has these dreams when she is feeling judged harshly at how she does something, and needs to improve her performance in that area.

A world-class opera singer sometimes dreams he is in the wrong costume in the wrong opera. This dream only happens when he is not feeling confident about a role. When he has this dream, he realizes he feels unprepared, speaks to the director, and arranges for extra rehearsal so he can perform with confidence. It's a good idea to use your dreams of poor performance to spur you into taking action that will help you do your best.

Peak Performance

You'll find it helpful to ask yourself these questions:

1. What person or situation is making me feel "tested" or "judged" right now?
2. How can I prepare myself better for doing well in this waking-life situation?

Remind yourself that you've taken many tests before and survived. Your dreams often picture the worst possibility. This gets your attention and encourages you to take action to improve the situation.

If your dream of poor performance involves not having the right equipment, consider what you feel is missing to do well in the waking world. Get some support in the area you lack confidence. Get coached. See about finding a tutor. Talk with friends who already know about this area of life. Read books on the subject. You'll be better equipped to deal with any test life might hand out.

Your dreams can also supply support. Occasionally you may have the pleasurable dream of doing really well. You may dream of acing an exam, just whizzing along knowing the right answers to a difficult test. You may dream about performing superbly in a play, musical, sport, or other competitive event. It seems easy and fun to do.

Whether you're sinking the winning basket in a dream game, shining as you sing in full voice, or winning the swim meet, you feel exhilarated and successful. You perform with confidence. Such dreams are a kind of practice in which you experience the smoothness of performing with ease. Arnold Schwarzenegger often dreamed of doing well and winning a weight-lifting contest the night before he was to compete. Athletes sometimes use mental rehearsal to improve their movements in their sport.

You're most likely to dream about a peak performance when you focus on the skill you want to develop. Imagine yourself experiencing your skill perfectly. In the drowsy state before you drift off to sleep, picture yourself doing what you want to do – sinking basketballs, dancing in *The Nutcracker*, painting the picture, playing the violin, scoring high on the test – smoothly and easily. Flow, ride the rhythm, glide gracefully. Feel yourself moving effortlessly. Give a great performance.

When you dream of performing well, whatever skill you wish to develop, really notice the sensations in your dream. Remember these sensations when you actually perform. You'll enrich your dreaming world as well as your waking one. You are preparing for success.

7

Help – I'm Falling!

"I am flying in an airplane to go skydiving. It's over a desert with lots of plateaus. I jump and feel the air flowing over me. It's great. I look down and see a small mesa. The desert is all red dirt and stuff, and I hit down. POW. All black. Then I'm back up in the airplane, and do it over and over. It's fun!!"

– Aric, 14

Falling in a dream is not usually as much fun as it was for this dreamer. Kids describe the terror of a rapid descent, the rush of wind as their body plummets, often through dark nothingness. Most hurl themselves awake in order to prevent collision with the ground. Some actually strike the floor by their bed as they startle awake. In addition to actual falls from bed, many people experience a falling sensation as they fall asleep.

Dreams of falling are one of the most common nightmares. Out of 100 kids surveyed, 63 percent said they had dreamed about falling. Although many kids said they had this nightmare more often when they were little, the number of older kids reporting the dream was almost exactly the same as the adults who had falling dreams (64 percent).

If you haven't already dreamed about falling, you probably will at some point. Such dreams are most likely to occur when you feel insecure or that you don't have enough emotional support.

Falling with Fear

The meaning of your dream of falling depends partly on how it ends up. Do you wrench yourself awake to avoid painful contact with the ground? Do you hit the ground and get hurt? Do you land safely without pain? Do you enjoy the impact? Do you transform the dream into carefree soaring?

When you are unable to change the dream fall, you have lost your solid footing for the time being. You feel helpless about some life change.

❋

To fall with fear in a dream is to feel insecure.

❋

You might feel at risk when starting school, changing to a new school, coping with a divorce in your family, or adjusting to a new sibling. Many younger kids describe dreams of frightening falls when something goes wrong in their waking life.

- A seven-year-old boy told me, "I dream I am in bed then all of a sudden I am falling through the air into a blackberry patch." Some painful "prickly" change must have recently entered his life.
- "I fall into a hole eight feet deep and have to eat dirt for a week." This boy was about to turn eight years old. He seemed to feel this change was unappetizing and would somehow trap him.
- An eleven-year-old girl dreamed she was swinging back and forth on a trapeze in a circus: "A friend of mine on the other trapeze is trying to catch me. So we are swinging back and forth. I let go and he is supposed to catch me but he misses." Someone in this girl's life must have recently let her down.

These dreams of falling continue as kids get older. A girl dreamed she was walking up a very steep wooded hillside when she started falling down the hill. She tried to grab trees to stop her tumble but couldn't hold on. "I kept falling and fell into the water that was forty feet deep and the edge was at a ninety-degree angle so I could not climb out. I ended up drowning in the dream and have been afraid of water ever since." This girl not only lost her foothold, but also became overwhelmed and felt unable to extricate herself. Her dream fear carried over to the waking world

If you have such a dream when something changes for the worse in your life, don't be alarmed. It's a normal reaction. Use the dream to alert yourself to how you feel at the moment. Find ways to restore your balance.

The Cliff Edge

Your dream about falling will often start from a high place. In fact, most dreamers start a falling dream from the edge of a cliff. This dream setting warns you that you feel on the brink of danger in some waking-life situation. Cliffs are a risky place to be.

Other dreams of falling begin at the edge of a roof, in an airplane, or on a tall building, a ladder, a staircase, a railing, a bridge, a roller coaster, or a Ferris wheel – all high places from which a fall could be deadly. However, some dreamers use these same locations from which to launch glorious dream flights.

If you dream about falling from any of these high places, take special care. Your dream is alerting you to the presence of danger in some waking situation. Don't slip into it; deal with it instead. Get help, talk with friends and relatives, get support. Get your feet back on the ground.

The Black Pit

You might dream of falling through black space, as lots of kids do. Plummeting down a black elevator shaft, or plunging through an endless pit, dreamers describe a dark nothingness around them that is nearly as frightening as the fall:

- I am in an elevator when the cable breaks.
- In my worst nightmare, I open a door, slip and fall into totally nothing, just space, pitch black.

Usually the darkness in such dreams refers to a temporary black mood, or not being able to see your way clearly out of a situation in which you feel helpless. As you begin to cope with whatever your problem is in waking life, light will return to your dreams as well as your waking hours.

Hitting Rock Bottom

Most falling dreams do not involve a fall to the floor. But one of my earliest dreams as a child was of riding in a small airplane when suddenly it loses power and spirals to earth with a great crash. I actually fell out of bed with this one. Many children tell me similar dreams that accompany a fall from bed:

- falling down a mountain
- falling off the Empire State Building
- being in a rocket that takes off in space.

It happens less often as you get older, but some older kids report dreams that go with a fall from bed:

- I jump off a diving board, but I don't hit the water, I hit the concrete at poolside.
- I'm Alice in Wonderland, falling down a hole after the rabbit, but really out of bed.

You might feel extremely frightened if you strike the ground in a falling dream. Maybe you've heard the folk saying that if you hit the ground in a dream you will die. It's not true. Lots of people survive the impact with dream earth.

Soft Landings

Dreams of falling aren't always scary. Maybe Aric's dream of having great fun hurling himself to earth let him experience the positive that can accompany the sensation of falling. Most kids who dream about falling don't realize it can be a pleasant dream, the start of an adventure.

If you have scary dreams of falling, remind yourself while you are awake that you can make a soft landing. In a dream, you can tell yourself to "fall gently and land gently" during the fall. Strange as it seems, this technique can change your dream. The trick is, of course, to remember it while you're dreaming. If you've fallen out of bed, this reminder won't cushion your floor, but it can make a big difference in recurrent bad dreams about falling.

A woman who was tortured by nightmares about driving over a cliff in a car changed her dream by telling herself, "Dr. Garfield says I don't have to crash." That night she had the same nightmare. As she fell, she reminded herself that she didn't have to let it happen. For the first time, she guided her car through the air and landed safely at the bottom of the cliff.

Some kids discover this soft landing technique for themselves. A girl dreamed she fell out of a building, but was unhurt because she landed on an old mattress. An eight-year-old girl dreamed of falling through a gutter where she found diamonds and other precious jewels at the bottom. Sometimes a life change that seems negative can lead to discovering something of value.

Changing Falling into Flying

Here are some questions to ask yourself after a dream about falling:

1. What situation have I "fallen into" lately that needs attention?
2. Who or what is making me feel "let down" recently?

3. What can I do about it? (There's always something positive to try.)
4. How can I restore my sense of balance and "lift myself" up again?

Surprisingly, one of the things you can do is become more aware in your dreams.

You can help yourself during a falling dream by transforming falling into flying. Some dreamers discover this ability for themselves; others learn it. By turning passive falling into active dream flying, you change more than your dream. You change your waking mood.

Eleven-year-old James dreamed "I am running and am trying to get somewhere. I trip over a stick and fall over a cliff, going down and down and I am almost about to hit the rocks. And I think . . . and I lift my body up and start flying. I'm over the house I just left. Birds start following me and talking and imitating me. I don't understand them but they fly forward and I follow them. A couple of eagles come and we are all flying and doing tricks and that. An airplane comes and I'm about to hit it so I wake up." Although the end of his dream included the danger of collision with the airplane, the boy succeeded in pulling out of a nasty fall in order to fly. And he didn't find that flying was scary: "No, I just did it. I was free, like a bird."

Dreamers like Aric and James discover the power of dream flight, the pleasure that dream flying can bring. And so can you.

8

Cool . . . I'm Flying!

"I dream I am a bird, a beautiful white egret flying in the clouds, and all these bluebirds are around. My feathers blow in the wind as I fly . . ."

— Lucy, 10

You dream of whizzing through space, feeling the wind, sensing incredible freedom. Flying is the all-time favorite dream for most people. Your dream flights might begin as an escape from near disaster. Or you might, like many dreamers, discover your ability to fly as you race to escape people pursuing you. Once you've flown in a dream, you're likely to keep the skill. Dream flight becomes a source of joy, especially when the sensation of flying feels incredibly real.

You're most likely to dream about joyous flying when things are going really well, when you feel that you have unlimited possibilities, can rise above your difficulties, and can get a wider perspective on your life. When you wake up from a dream of flying, you might feel in a better mood for days afterward.

In dreams we have the almost magical ability to fly like birds. Lucy's dream was unusual, since dreamers usually picture themselves flying with the birds, rather than being one. Her dream ended with her being put on top of a flying castle where she was given a spell by angels. For Lucy, bluebirds were associated with happiness. Her happiness came from being chosen for the lead in a school musical.

If we feel insecure and helpless in falling dreams, we feel free in flying ones. We can move in any direction of our choice, usually up. If you fly in your dreams, you know what delight it can bring.

❋

To fly in a dream is to feel free to achieve your waking wishes.

❋

While falling dreams tend to take place after a sense of failure, flying dreams are apt to arise when we feel successful. Did you ace the last exam? Get the part-time job you wanted? Win the part in the school play? Score the winning basket? Make a date with the person you like best? These and other achievements may be expressed in happy dream flight.

Early Flights

Dreams of flying start early in life. Children as young as five years old have flying dreams:

- I jump out of the car window and fly up into the sky, as high as the rockets go.
- I am flying like a bird while the moon is shining and some birds are also awakened and flying with me.

Older kids also report jubilant dreams of flight. Most adults have fewer flying dreams, but they treasure those that they do have.

Flying Styles

Your flying style is as personal as your fingerprint. Some dreamers hover in the air, some glide along upright a few feet above the ground. Others push off from the ground, as if from the bottom of a pool, to soar above the earth. For some dreamers, flying is like swimming:

- paddling on my back, propelling myself through space with hand and leg movements
- swimming in the air, floating on an inner tube across the heights
- swimming through the air using the breaststroke, going twenty feet with one pull.

You might use a mixture of styles, different ones in different dreams.

Many people fly facedown gazing with amazement at the landscape passing underneath. Others face upwards as they ascend through outer realms toward the moon. Some dreamers invent special flying outfits, like a particular nightgown or cape. All share a special exultation as they glide through space.

Flying Obstacles

Once in a great while a dreamer will lose power and fall back to earth while flying. Sometimes they worry about flying into overhead wires or other obstacles, or have a rough landing.

These occasional glitches in the best of dreams are usually overcome on the next dream flight. They often represent temporary obstacles in our waking-life space. Don't be discouraged if you encounter a problem from time to time. Recapture the sensation of flight in your mind's eye and you'll soon be soaring without limits. You already know how to fly!

Taking Flight

Some people value dream flight so much, they try to fly more often in their dreams. Thinking about flying, imagining yourself flying as you drift in the drowsy period before sleep can sometimes bring on dreams of flight. If you want to dream about flying, watch birds in flight to help you concentrate on the subject. You may also want to put your wish into a short phrase such as "tonight I fly"; repeat this to yourself rhythmically as you go to sleep.

Researchers find that dream imagery becomes more bizarre as the night progresses. Flying dreams are sometimes the final dreams of the night. Sleep more; dream more; fly more.

High Hopes

On one level, your dreams about flying high represent your ambition, your wish to succeed. The many kids who dream about flying want to have the power to save others, to be special, to do good deeds, and be rewarded. Boys and girls dream about flying like Superman or Wonder Woman to rescue those in danger. These dreams of flight may be the beginnings of the need to achieve and be appreciated.

But dream flight is more than ambition and pleasure with accomplishment. There is an ancient belief that when people dream of flying, their souls are literally traveling in spirit worlds. Many myths depict gods and goddesses as living in high places. Religious structures have most often been built on high ground in an attempt to get closer to the gods, the better for prayers to reach them. Some deities were supposed to have the power of flight, including Mercury, the Roman messenger of the gods (Hermes to the Greeks), who flew by means of wings on his helmet and sandals.

In our dreams of flight we may be reaching for something higher in ourselves. Perhaps when you dream about flying you are expressing more than success of the moment. Perhaps you are reaching for the stars and beyond, for your highest self.

9

Yikes! I'm Naked!

"I'm running through the halls at school wearing only a big diaper."

– Taryn, 14

The first time you dream of being naked in public, it's a real shocker. Suddenly you realize you are nude or only partly dressed in a public place, often school. You feel alarmed at the discovery you're undressed and want to escape, quickly. Or you may show up at an event wearing totally wrong clothes, such as pajamas in your math class. Being naked or wrongly dressed is a common nightmare.

When you dream of being naked in public, you'll probably feel embarrassed – the usual reaction. Some dreamers, especially if they've had the dream before, may not care, or even feel proud of the way their bodies look. A few dreamers feel free without their clothes. Mostly, however, kids are grossed out by this dream. They run, try to hide, or attempt to borrow or buy clothes to cover their bodies.

Why would you put yourself through this ordeal in dreams when you would never dream of doing it in the waking state?

❋

To be undressed in a dream is to feel emotionally exposed.

❋

Without our clothes, our social status and public presentation is stripped away; we feel vulnerable or inadequate. About 40 percent of kids said they'd had this dream; about 50 percent of adults reported having it.

Naked Spaces

To understand your dreams about being naked in public, notice where they take place.

At School Kids are most likely to dream about being naked at school, a natural spot for them to be and one in which they are sometimes emotionally vulnerable:

- I go to school completely naked and I am so embarrassed.
- I am in school without a shirt so a girl gives me hers.
- I am naked at school during an assembly.
- I'm naked at school and the teacher asks me to do a problem at the board but I'm too embarrassed.

The place you find yourself nude or partly dressed in a dream gives you a clue to the area of your life where you feel vulnerable. If you dream about being naked at school, you may be feeling vulnerable to the opinions of classmates or teachers.

In the Bathroom The second most common place you might dream about being naked is in the bathroom, taking a bath or going to the toilet. Although the bathroom seems a normal place to be naked, in dreams with this setting kids often mention being observed by someone else:

- I'm naked on parents' night and have to take a shower while my father and my French teacher discuss my work.
- Before I get to the bathroom, my pants drop in front of people.
- I'm taking a bath in front of my house with a hose.

If you have a dream like this, you can be fairly sure that something in your waking life that's usually private feels too exposed and public for comfort. The girl who dreamed her father and French teacher were discussing her work while she was naked in the shower was probably feeling anxious about some aspect of her school performance.

At the Beach or Pool You might dream about being nude at the beach or at a pool, other places where the body is usually more exposed than where people wear regular clothes:

- I'm playing billiards on a tropical beach in my underwear.
- I'm naked in a swimming pool, but I win the swim competition.
- I go swimming naked and have sex in the pool.

Any dream about being naked can be positive if you are feeling comfortable or happy or successful. Winning the swim competition while nude suggests the dreamer is feeling confident about her body and her ability to achieve.

Other Settings Other kids dream they are walking down the street nude, or are naked in the center of town, at a party, or in the living room with strangers. One boy dreamed he was naked in ski class, feeling very cold. Wherever your naked dreams are set, you are likely to be wondering how other people are judging you – your body, general appearance, or skills.

Reactions Reveal Emotions

How do you react in your dream to being naked? The emotions you have during the dream will tell you how you feel about being emotionally exposed.

1. Are you filled with shame? Deeply embarrassed? You are likely to feel that people are judging you harshly.
2. Do you try to hide? You're uncomfortable with what you've revealed to others. You'd probably like to conceal any weakness you think you have.
3. Do you borrow clothes? Try to buy some? If people help you and lend you clothing, or you're able to find or buy some, you feel more capable of dealing with the momentary vulnerability.
4. Do you feel indifferent? You're apt to be more comfortable with revealing intimate feelings.

5. Do you enjoy being nude in your dream? Feel proud? You probably are confident about your body, or your role in life. You may want others to appreciate your appearance and abilities.
6. Do you feel uninhibited and free? Perhaps you feel good about being more emotionally open in some waking-life relationship.

How do other people in your dream react to your vulnerability? Do they laugh at and mock you? Do they ignore you? Try to help? Admire you? The way others react in your dream of being naked in public will tell you what *you* think people think about you.

Some Clothes On, Some Clothes Off

If you dream that part of your clothing is missing, notice what area of your body is exposed. The exposed area in your dream helps you understand where you feel especially vulnerable at the moment. Girls who dream about being without blouses, being topless, or wearing only bras are often concerned about their breast size or if other people find them attractive. Boys who dream about being without pants may be concerned about how their masculine strength compares to other males.

Many dreamers are missing shoes and socks. If you have this dream, you may be feel you don't have proper protection in an emotional situation in waking life. Your feet get you where you want to go. When they are bare in a dream, you have lost protection and are feeling at risk of not being able to move freely in your waking-life space.

Adolescence is a strange time, when you have one foot in childhood and the other in adulthood. You still want to be taken care of and protected. At the same time you want to be free to do whatever you want. When you dream of being partly dressed or of missing essential items of clothing, you express these mixed feelings as you prepare to cross the border into adulthood.

Fashion Crimes

The wrong clothing in dreams often consists of nightclothes or underwear in school or other places where such attire would be inappropriate. Such dreams suggest the dreamer may be acting in a way that is too intimate or is more personal than is desirable in some waking situation.

Taryn's dream (which starts this chapter) of running down the hallway wearing only a big diaper was probably telling her that she was behaving childishly in some waking situation at school. A dream like this can be a strong message to yourself to grow up and act your age. Another girl dreamed that she was the only one in school who was dressed, while everyone else laughed at her for wearing clothes. Was she feeling pressured to reveal more of herself than she was ready to do in a waking situation?

Your dreams tell you how you feel *at the moment of the dream.* Years or months or even weeks later, you will probably feel very different about the same facts. To understand how you feel right now, ask yourself exactly what is wrong about the clothing in your dream.

1. Is the clothing too small? You may feel that your body is too big, or maybe you wish it were bigger. You might be feeling restricted by your current waking life and want more personal space.

2. Clothing too big? You may feel that your body is too little. Or maybe you feel you can't fill your role in current waking life, that it's too much for you.

3. Do your clothes have clashing patterns or colors? Something in your waking life is as clashing as plaids worn with polka dots.

4. Is your clothing age-inappropriate? Are you acting childishly in a waking situation?

5. Are your clothes too weird? What's going on in your waking state that feels wacky right now?

6. Are they out-of-style? You probably feel that something you're doing or thinking is too old-fashioned.

7. Too formal? Too casual? You feel your behavior is inappropriate for some waking situation.

Dreams of wearing the wrong clothing suggest that you have some conflict about your body or your role in life at the time of the dream. Your dream clothing may be screaming the message: "You don't have the right equipment you need!" But remember that your body will change over time, and so will your feelings and dreams about it. The clothing you wear – or don't wear – in your dreams can teach you how you feel about your body now and how you feel you compare to classmates and friends. Sometimes, your dream wardrobe says that you're doing great!

10

Looking Good

"The popular girl in school is wearing a pink dress with pink bows, looking sweet."

— Anya, 15

If your dreams about being half-dressed or wearing weird clothes tell you about your areas of weakness, dreams about beautiful clothes and stylish outfits reveal growing strengths. In bad clothing dreams, your outfits don't fit, or are mismatched, weird, or absent. In good clothing dreams, things fit perfectly, are harmonious, flattering, and fun. Good clothing dreams e-mail your waking self messages that you feel good about your body, that your confidence is high, and that you're pleased with your current life role.

You're likely to smile when you wake up from a dream about being well dressed. You may admire the style, the fabric, the comfort, or the color of your dream outfit. Maybe it's the latest thing from your favorite store or it's a special outfit for the school dance. It could be a wedding gown, a suit, a regal robe, or a religious or military uniform. You wear whatever delights your dreaming mind to portray yourself feeling pleased and being admired.

These dreams are more than wishes for a particular outfit. They express hopes for better bodies, better health, or better life roles, or they express happiness at achieving these goals. Good clothing dreams are often expressions of growing confidence. You'll have them when you're feeling upbeat.

❋

To be well dressed in a dream is to feel
good about your body and your life role.

❋

Clothes Make the Dreamer

What's hanging in your dream closet? It could be something attractive for school. Maybe it's a special-occasion outfit for a dance or wedding. Perhaps it's swimwear that shows off your body. Might it be a costume, or some totally imaginary outfit? Each says something about your body or your current waking role.

Twelve-year-old Asha dreamed "I saw that Daddy has come from Bombay and has brought many dresses for me. I am very happy." It would be easy to dismiss this dream as wishful thinking, but it is more than that. Asha is becoming a woman. Her father's gift of dresses is a gift of maturity – one the dreamer yearns for and feels ready to "wear" soon.

Fourteen-year-old Dani dreamed about going shopping with her father. "I was walking down the street with Dad and someone else. We stopped to look in a store window at white and black purses. Dad said, 'Let's go in and look at some for you.' We went in." This dream, too, suggests the father's approval for the girl to accept herself as an attractive young woman. Purses in dreams are often symbols for the role of being a woman.

Anya (whose dream starts this chapter) thought of pink as an especially feminine color. The popular girl was very curvaceous and attractive to boys, and Anya envied her. Her dream shows she wanted to look as cute and appealing. Anya was not yet wearing the super-feminine outfit herself, but the fact that she dreamed about it suggests she felt hopeful she would in the near future.

Girls dream more about clothing than boys do, from very early ages. As they grow older and more aware of their sexual attractiveness, they have more of these dreams. Little girls' dreams are filled with bridal gowns and princess robes.

But boys dream about clothes, too:

- I'm wearing a Superman outfit.
- I'm dressed in the uniform of the captain of the starship Enterprise from *Star Trek*.
- I've got on Batman's costume.
- I'm all dressed in this cool *Matrix* black outfit ready to fight and all. I'm fighting a guy who's bald and shirtless and buff. I take off my sunglasses and throw them aside, then pull off my trench coat and throw it at him. We start to fight, like with martial arts.

These dreams are not just longing for a Halloween costume. The dreaming boys want to be strong, important, and heroic in the eyes of their friends. They want to become men.

Perfect Fit

Your dream clothing is an expression of your feelings about your physical body. More than two thousand years ago, the Greek doctor Hippocrates, the father of medicine, noticed this connection. He said that when people are well, "the person's dream clothing and footwear appear attractive, and in the right size, neither too large nor too small." That's still true.

Pregnant women often dream about trying on dresses that are too tight. They also dream about shopping for larger clothes. When people have gained weight, in pregnancy or otherwise, they may dream about thick or restrictive clothes. When weight is lost healthfully, people have dreams of peeling off layers of clothing until they get down to a well-fitting outfit. Some dream of wearing slinky bathing suits as their natural body shape emerges.

A grossly overweight young woman was scheduled to have her gallbladder removed. She dreamed of receiving some old material to cut apart and sew into a new dress for a bridal gown. She hoped not only for a slimmer body after surgery (a new dress cut out of old material), but also for love and marriage to go with it.

Women recovering from surgery often dream of beautiful clothes and accessories:

- exquisite wedding gowns
- designer outfits
- marvelous jewelry

Dreams about such attractive clothing can reflect restored health.

Royal Powers

One boy told about a dream in which he wears a king's hat. And girls often dream about dressing like princesses. Part of the appeal of these dreams is not simply the rich costumes the dreamer gets to wear; it's the power they put on with the clothing.

When Patti was fourteen, she dreamed of being a lady named Wilhelmina (Wilhelmina was a queen of the Netherlands. Perhaps this is a dream pun on the word "me" to point out that the dreamer was playing the role). She wears handsome flowing robes. Suddenly a messenger on a white horse arrives with the news that she has been named the heir to the throne of the Queen of England. Everyone bows and tries to please her. One of her first decisions is to execute two slaves, who in reality were two boys who constantly teased Patti at school. Certainly, Patti would have liked to have the royal power to eliminate them from her life!

Dreaming Heads

What you wear on your head in a dream tells you what you are thinking about, even if you don't realize you're thinking it. Dreamers sometimes shop for hats in their dreams when they are considering different points of view. Trying on hats or shopping for any dream clothing suggests the dreamer is considering options and making life choices. A girl dreamed "My hair has streaks of pink, blue, or purple." She was testing some different ways of thinking. What dream hats or hairstyles do you wear?

Your clothing is a kind of second skin. In your dreams, your good-looking, harmonious outfit indicates good feelings about your figure or your present role in life. It may tell you about improvements in health or attitude, or give you an individual message. Let your dream wardrobe teach you. You may find an outfit you want to wear every day of your life.

11

Disaster Strikes

"Fire is falling from the sky. Lava is everywhere. The earth quakes."

— Dewi, 18

If you dream about being in a natural disaster or being in a war zone, you'll probably wake up as shaken as Dewi was from her nightmare. Your catastrophic dream may involve rushing to escape a flood or tidal wave. Maybe you're in the middle of a volcanic eruption, or fleeing from lava, a firestorm, or a lightning strike. The ground beneath you might split apart in an earthquake. A tornado, typhoon, or hurricane may howl around you. Kids have had dreams about nuclear attacks, holocausts, World War III, chemical attacks, acid rain, mustard gas, napalm, and other explosive and toxic nightmares.

Your dreams might be filled with chaos and violence. As with all nightmares, these dreams get our attention. They force us to hear the message: "Alert! Alert! Things are in bad shape at the moment. Do something."

Dreams about upheavals of nature can be the most frightening dreams ever. To many dreamers, it feels like the end of the world has arrived. Dreams exaggerate and overdramatize. The circumstances of our waking lives are usually not as serious as they are pictured in our dreams of catastrophes. But we need to understand the dream images and use them to improve our waking situation. You saw in chapter 1 "Oh No, It's After Me!" that when some annoying person or situation plagues you, you might dream about being chased or attacked. When you feel as if your life is coming apart, you are more likely to dream about a widespread catastrophe.

❋

To dream about a disaster is to feel in a personal waking crisis.

❋

Dreams about disasters are fairly common. Nearly 40 percent of kids said they had disaster dreams, and most of them had these nightmares often.

The place where you live might be in danger of certain types of calamities. Do you live in an earthquake belt? Is your area periodically struck by a hurricane? Do tidal waves loom near the coast where you live? Are tornadoes common in your part of the world? The physical storms in your environment become the likeliest pictures of personal emotional storms in your nightmares.

When people live in war zones, or when tragedies such as terrorist attacks occur close to home, people are even more likely to dream about similar situations. And, with the TV news, radio emergency bulletins, and Internet captions, we are becoming more aware of disasters and warfare in places far from our homes. These can become symbols of personal crises in our dreams.

Each nightmare has something to teach you about your inner emotions. Frightening as they may be, these dreams can help you develop your abilities to cope with the crisis in your waking world.

Natural Disasters

Feeling Shaken

Whether or not you have actually gone through an earthquake, you may dream about one when events in your life are in turmoil. These dreams point to a change in your life, one that seems dangerous. Like Dewi, some dreamers fear being burned from fire, hurt by falling debris, and falling into an abyss that opens in the cracking earth.

In general, earthquake dreams are often puns for a situation in your life that is coming apart or breaking up. Is there a divorce, a split, taking place in your family? Are you breaking up with a boyfriend or girlfriend? Are your grades falling apart?

Destruction in an earthquake dream usually represents your fears of emotional damage. However, sometimes earthquake and volcano dreams are signs that your physical or psychological health is getting bad. This is rare, but if you suspect this might be true for you, get some professional advice from your doctor or counselor.

If you have this type of disaster dream, you probably know what waking-life situation it represents. But it's important to ask yourself what feels at risk right at this moment. Remember that situations change.

Did you do anything in your dream to escape the destruction that was underway? Seventeen-year-old Hal dreamed about floods, world wars, and nuclear holocausts, but he saw people as disappearing rather than dying: "The world becomes a survivalist social structure where I excel and thrive." Taking positive action in dreams can help you feel more able to cope with the waking-life situation as well as the dream. Saving yourself and others in disaster nightmares is desirable.

Is there any possible benefit from the change going on in your waking life? Time may show you that what seems unbearable at the moment might become a benefit in the future. Look for it.

Great Waters

If you dream about floods and tidal waves, you are probably telling yourself in vivid pictures that things are overwhelming; it's too much.

When you dream a tidal wave is about to crash down on you, or that floodwaters surround you, or torrents of rain hit you, you are likely to wake up scared. Such dreams occur when we feel overwhelmed, even hopeless. The girl who dreamed "There was a flood in my backyard" felt the threat to her well-being was close to home. Dreams about great waters often stand for feelings of great sadness, tears of despair. They often occur in emotional crises. They express the dreamer's feeling of being in an emergency.

At times, nightmares of great waters arise when there is a physical cause. Certain physical conditions are accompanied by the accumulation of excess water within the body. Many people dream of overwhelming waters when they have colds, bronchitis, or pneumonia. One woman with pneumonia dreamed she was drowning in an upside-down submarine. Such dreams will stop as the person gets better. A man who had suffered three heart attacks had a dream about surviving three tidal waves. He stands on a cliff watching the huge waves approach. He fears being swept off the cliff into the deep waters. Although the third tidal wave swirls around his ankles, the water recedes. His dream combined the emotional threat of being overwhelmed with the physical water retention that patients with heart conditions often have.

Dreams about excess water are a normal response to feeling overwhelmed and sad about some situation.

Did you make an effort to help yourself in the dream? You don't have to get in over your head. A girl had dreams of seeing an immense tidal wave approaching, but it did not always reach her. A woman in a difficult marriage had dreams of being swept away by raging waters. In her dreams, she struggles to cling to trees and save herself. Finally, in one of her dreams, she manages to swim to an island and safety. The fact that she managed to survive in the last dream gave her greater strength to deal with the painful waking situation her dream represented.

Whatever type of turmoil or sadness you may be currently experiencing, remember how important it is to take positive action. It may seem strange to try to change your dream, but with practice it can work. Remind yourself as you fall asleep to try to make any bad dream better. While you're awake, think about your dream and what it might mean. Imagine yourself staying afloat, swimming, breathing, surviving. Time may improve the waking situation. You can get support. Coping with your nightmare helps you grow and develop. You can move away from it toward joyful new adventures.

Disaster Strikes

Great Winds

If you dream that a tornado is coming, like many kids do, you are warning yourself about an emotional storm on the horizon. Wind was once thought to be the breath of a god or goddess, bringing divine creations to life. Fierce winds, along with thunderbolts and lightning, were believed to be the god's anger. When you dream about destructive wind, you might be feeling blown away by strong emotions:

- I am under attack from a satanic being and there are earthquakes, eruptions, wild storms, and black lightning.
- There is a tornado outside my window. I'm on an island vacation and a flood comes. Horses are dying. Monkeys are being chopped up.

What is making you feel storm-tossed at the moment? Is there something in your present life that feels as if it's "gone with the wind"?

Did you take action in your dream to protect yourself or others from the overpowering winds? Remember that in dreams you might be able to ride the wind, and fly high over troubled waters to safe harbors. Absorb the energy of your dream whirlwinds to help you deal with your waking-life difficulties. Perhaps these are the winds of change for you. They can bring something new and positive into your life.

Volcanic Eruptions and Firestorms

If your disaster dream involves fire or volcanic eruptions, as it did in Dewi's dream at the start of this chapter, it is probably expressing feelings of anger in other people or in you. A dream about a volcanic eruption is often a dream pun for explosive anger.

Many cultures have worshipped fire for its warmth, as protection from wild beasts, and for cooking food. But destructive fire – lightning strikes and volcanic eruptions – was thought to be the fury of an angry god or goddess. The burning ash and lava, destroying crops, livestock, homes, and villagers, were believed to be a punishment.

In dreams, fire is often associated with one of three conditions: anger, passion, or physical inflammation. When you dream about firestorms or volcanic explosions, any of these three conditions may be involved.

Anger Our language is filled with references to the heat of angry feelings – "I'm burned up"; "I'm about to blow up"; "I'm seeing red." In dreams, these words become vivid images of volcanic explosions, rushing lava, and burning towns. Did your teacher criticize you unfairly? Did a parent explode in fury at you? Did a close friend burst out with remarks that made you "burn"? Has there been a destructive quarrel recently in your waking life? Anger in real life results in dream damage by fire:

• The sun comes into the earth's atmosphere and kills everyone.
• Airplanes are dropping lava onto people's houses.

The damage caused in dreams about fire expresses the emotional damage you or other people experienced as a result of rage.

Passion We also use images of fire to express feelings of love and desire. We may describe an attractive person as a hottie, or say we are hot for someone. In dreams, these statements become literal. Many teenagers dream about houses or buildings on fire when they feel the heat of passion. A girl from England dreamed about volcanoes, the sky filled with rusty colors, with wildfires and a "hot fence" surrounding her and her friends. Was she feeling protected from violent anger around her, or was she dangerously close to runaway passion? Such fiery images picture both the warmth of desire and the risk of getting hurt in a close relationship. Don't be surprised to see the flames of passion light your dreamscape. It's a natural reaction.

Inflammation and Fever Dreams about fire can result from excessive heat in your body. People with headaches sometimes dream about their hair being on fire. Children who were victims of severe burns drew pictures of scorching sun and summer beaches with burning sand, echoing the burning sensations on their skins. As the dreamer's health returns, there are often dreams about buildings being repaired or new ones being constructed.

Sometimes, dream fires stand for more than one of these things. Once my wrist was badly injured from a break that was misdiagnosed as a sprain. It took extensive surgery to rebreak the wrongly aligned bones and insert screws to hold them in place. The night before surgery I had a vivid nightmare that I was in a city where a huge fire is burning. People panic, afraid of being trapped by the fire. I take refuge in an underground cave and, although I can hear a gigantic explosion on the surface, I survive safely under the earth. This dream dramatized both the heat in my inflamed wrist and the furious anger I felt toward the doctor who had made the misdiagnosis.

Whenever you dream about destructive fire, ask yourself if anger, passion, or physical heat is the cause. Find ways to beat down or redirect the fire in your dreams as well as in your waking situation. Understanding yourself helps you make better decisions.

Big Freeze

At times the problem in our dreams is not too much heat but too much cold. Dreams of ice and snow, hail, and wintry freeze often stand for waking-life chilly emotions that numb the dreamer. When you dream about bitter cold in any form, you might be portraying frigid emotions in some other person or in yourself.

Emotional Freezes A girl dreamed that her girlfriend slips on ice and, when she gets up, her whole head has turned into a block of ice. Her dream suggests that the girlfriend "slipped up" in some way and that her own reaction was to become icy cold to her. A woman who was grieving the death of her son dreamed he comes to her and helps her throw rocks into a frozen river so the water can flow again. She hugs him and asks why he has come. He says, "Oh, Mom, I thought you needed some help to break up the ice in your heart." The woman awoke, able to shed tears. She felt encouraged by this dream in which her deceased son helped her. If you dream about frozen land or water or people, you probably feel frozen by some person or situation in waking life and need to allow yourself to flow freely.

Physical Freezes Parts of the body may feel abnormally cold when there is restricted circulation. When my wrist was broken, my ring and little fingers were cold and numb because a nerve was compressed. In a dream during this time, I am driving through an area with ice-covered trees. The tiniest branches are coated with ice, and the wind blowing through them makes an eerie sound. Suddenly the car jams. I am afraid to be stuck in this cold awful place. Here my dream compared my chilly fingers to ice-covered twigs. The wail of the wind was probably my moan of fear.

If you should dream about cold, assess whether the source of the dream is from chilly emotions in your waking environment or from a physical cause. Are you feeling cold and loveless? Frozen with grief? Icy with fear? Find ways to melt the ice and cold in your dreams. Think about how to thaw out icy feelings and invite warm loving ones into your life.

Living in a War Zone

Mankind has created disasters to equal and sometimes exceed the upheavals of nature. Kids often dream they are suffering the effects of a war.

If you dream about war, you are probably going through some hard times in the waking state. When heavy quarrels go on and on, kids sometimes get weary from explosive anger in those around them or disgusted with their own eruptions of fury. It feels like a state of war:

- I try to escape gas attacks and acid rain.
- People spray mustard gas or napalm into the air, setting the market and my house on fire.
- Mom and I are in a house when someone yells over a loudspeaker to evacuate, then there's a bomb blast and we're thrown into the air.
- I'm in a battlefield when I see a man fall out of a plane, people are running, an old man being beaten, tanks appear.
- There's a nuclear holocaust.

The poisonous gases and other toxins in these dreams usually refer to the noxious effects on the dreamer of angry arguments or feelings. Some dreamers see themselves walking through rubble and the remains after a major disaster. When dreamers explore the ruins of the aftermath of a war or manmade disaster, they are surveying emotional damage caused by the waking-life turmoil.

A girl dreamed of being a sergeant in Vietnam who has been shot and left on a hillside to die. She thought she might be reliving a past life. A boy described his dream about an invasion of Atlantis that destroys the city by fire. There is no way to know whether such dreams are truly past-life memories, but we can be sure they are expressions of chaos currently taking place in the dreamer's life. When we dream about warfare, we act out the struggle of humans to rise above anger and hate. We are battling the flaws in ourselves, and in the people and circumstances that surround us.

If you dream about war, it's a good idea to review any angry feelings you have at the moment, or think about any anger aimed at you. Remember the importance of attempting to protect yourself and others when you study your dreams. Imagine ways to get help, to save yourself and others if you can. Think over how to resolve or cope with the waking situation the dream represents. Is there anything you might learn from this period of inner or outer conflict? If you are in danger from an actual war, you probably can't change these circumstances in waking life. However, if you try, you might be able to change your dreams about it.

When inner calm returns, dreams can show us scenes of overwhelming beauty. You may wander through lush gardens or blossoming trees, bathe in healing waters, be touched by warm sunshine, feel a cooling breeze, or watch spectacular sunsets and moonrises. Perhaps you will glide down ski slopes with pleasure, swim in underwater grottos, or join in a round dance. Such dreams are sometimes accompanied by heavenly music. At times we are gifted with dreams of beauty during a personal crisis. They support and encourage us. Whenever dreams of beauty come to you, welcome them.

12

I'm Stuck in Muck

"I'm trapped in a room with no windows as it begins to fill with water."

– Olivia, 15

If you dream about being lost, feeling desperate as you try to find your way out of a dangerous city area, a forest, or a maze-like building, you will probably wake up feeling extremely frustrated. Some dreamers tell me about being buried alive, being caught in a web, or locked in a cage.

Many dreamers speak of escaping some evil thing in pursuit, while their legs feel as heavy as if they are trying to run through water, mud, or wet cement. Occasionally, you may dream that you are unable to move, feeling paralyzed, perhaps unable to scream or even breathe. A few people awaken still feeling trapped in their bodies, a condition called "sleep paralysis."

As you get older, you are trying to find your way to becoming an adult. However different our goals may be, we all struggle to find our way in life. From time to time we get confused, puzzled, and unsure of which way to turn. That's why so many kids dream about being lost or trapped. They have nightmares of being lost or trapped at exactly the same rate as adults do (58 percent), which shows that grown-ups get confused, too.

❋

To be lost or trapped in a dream is to
feel confused or conflicted in waking life.

❋

Lost and Found

If you dream that you are lost, you are probably feeling confused about what to do in some waking situation. You might be puzzled about your math assignment or mystified why some former friend is no longer speaking to you, or maybe you just don't know what to do about an unpleasant situation in your home.

Ask yourself the following questions to help you solve your puzzle:

1. Where was I trying to go? Home? School? Music Lesson? Work?
2. Where did I get lost?
3. What got me off the path?
4. What did I do in the dream to help myself find the way?
5. What feels confusing in my waking life at the moment?

Your goal in the dream – home, school, or some other place – gives you a clue to the meaning of your dream. The place you are trying to reach in a dream of being lost represents the goal that is hard to grasp.

One girl had recurrent dreams about getting lost on the way to her piano teacher. She felt guilty for not practicing enough and was reluctant to go. At the same time, she wanted to develop her skill at the piano, a goal that eluded her in the dream world as well as in the waking one. Another girl had been forced to transfer from one high school to another during her junior year because her parents moved to a different area. She never felt at home in the new school. It was hard to make friends and fit in with classmates who had been together for years. In addition, her parents' marriage became troubled. She often dreamed of getting lost trying to find her old high school. It was more than the former school she wanted. Her desire was to recapture the feeling of security and peace she had in that former time.

Sometimes kids are just lost, with no particular goal other than to get out:

- I am lost in a haunted house.
- I am lost in a weird unfamiliar place.
- I am lost in a building.

If you dream about being lost in a house or building with endless hallways, doors that open to more halls, places that seem to lead nowhere, you'll feel as if you're inside a maze with no exit. These dreams suggest a more general confusion and uncertainty than those dreams where you are headed home or some other specific place. You might feel that you are making no progress in solving a waking problem.

Many dreams of being lost take place in darkness. Perhaps you dream of being lost in dangerous dark city streets, or on country roads with no streetlights or guideposts, or in the desert at night. These dark conditions represent the difficulty you have in seeing the way clearly in the waking situation that puzzles you.

Caught in a Trap

You will often feel worse in dreams about being trapped than in those of being lost. Your space and your possibilities of escape are more restricted:

- I am trapped in my closet.
- I am trapped in a room.
- I am trapped in a maze.
- I am trapped by a wire metal boundary.
- I am trapped in an underground room beneath Wal-Mart, screaming hard but no one comes.
- I am trapped by others who tie me up to prevent my escape.

Places of entrapment, like places where dreamers are lost, are often dark. Inside a closet, under the earth, inside a sinking ship – the blackness of these spots may stand for a "black" mood as well as how hard it is to see your way. When you are trapped in a dream, you are probably experiencing a dilemma about something in your waking life. Where you are trapped often tells you something about the area of waking life in which you feel stuck.

Your reaction in a dream of being trapped is important. One girl dreamed "I am trapped on a ship with other people. I try to find them, but I can't because the ship starts to sink. Water is crashing everywhere." Her dream might have been about an overwhelming family situation that was getting worse. It might have been a school situation that she felt unable to survive. Whatever the case, the fact that she tried to find other people is a good sign. Although it failed in this dream, she made an effort and could perhaps succeed in future dreams or waking situations.

Even better is the response of the girl who dreamed "I am trapped underwater, but I have an oxygen tank." She, too, was in an overwhelming situation, but had supplied herself in the dream with the means of survival. She was feeling more hopeful about her ability to cope with her waking-life problem.

In her dream at the beginning of this chapter, Olivia feels hopeless as well as trapped and terrified. She described no attempt to escape. Yet many kids who dream they are trapped in water make the marvelous discovery that they are able to breathe underwater. Their fear pushes them to discover inner strength to survive.

If you dream about being trapped, try to escape. Your struggle to cope with the elements in the nightmare will give you greater ability to cope with the waking situation your dream represents. Trying to save yourself and others, getting rescued, or finding you have equipment or magical powers that can help you is far better than giving up.

Trapped in Your Body

The most unpleasant form the nightmare of being trapped takes is that of being partially or totally paralyzed:

- I am paralyzed and can't breathe or speak.
- I can hardly move my legs to escape.
- I'm running but it feels as if I'm running in tar.
- I feel like I'm crawling, unable to talk or scream.
- I'm paralyzed, being smothered by something or someone I'm unable to push away.
- I can't move; I'm suffocating in what feels like a blanket.

Slow Motion Running

You may share with many dreamers the peculiar sensation of running in slow motion as you try to escape in a dream. Researchers think this strange feeling comes from the fact that dreamers are usually unable to move their large muscles while dreaming. A special body mechanism turns on to protect the dreamer from acting out dreams. When this mechanism does not work, people walk in their sleep. So if you feel as if you are running through water, or thick mud, or wet cement, it's actually normal. When you have to force yourself to make strenuous efforts to move your legs as you escape a dream villain, it's your body's way of protecting you from starting to run in your sleep.

These dreams suggest that the dreamer feels, for the moment, totally unable to cope with the waking situation that entraps them. If you cannot run in a dream, you feel unable to get away from the waking-life difficulty. If you cannot speak or scream in the dream, you feel unable to get help while awake. If you can't breathe in the dream, you may feel your life is at risk. If you feel heavy-legged in the dream, you feel weighted down by the waking situation.

Sleep Paralysis

The dreadful feeling of being paralyzed may persist when you wake up. This condition is called sleep paralysis, and it can terrify the person who experiences it. Awake, eyes open, yet unable to move or make a sound, people feel as if they are in a trance. Sometimes the dreamer can see the figure of an animal or a dangerous person in the room, at the foot of the bed or on his or her chest. People feel as if an evil spell possesses them. In olden times people believed a witch called a "night hag" caused the sensation of weight or pressure on the chest.

One boy dreamed "A dark dog/creature is sitting on my chest about to bite off my face." He struggles to throw it off, to find it turns into his younger brother; they fight and the dreamer is killed. A young woman dreamed that a huge boulder was pressing down on her and other people. Another spoke of getting heavier and heavier, sinking through the bed. These dreams are typical of the feelings of sleep paralysis.

Sleep specialists tell us that this condition is caused by a malfunction of the nervous system, in which the mind wakes up before the body does. When a person has sleep paralysis, that mechanism that stops your large muscles from moving while you are asleep is still active, rather than turning off as it usually does. Researchers say the condition can be brought on by a meal of heavy carbohydrates.

If you have an episode of sleep paralysis, stay calm. The condition always passes, usually in a few minutes. Fright can prolong it. Remind yourself that it will go away soon. Try wiggling small parts of your body, such as your toes and fingers. Move your eyes in different directions; they are not affected. Breathe evenly and deeply. Soon you'll be able to move normally. If the sleep paralysis was brought on by eating carbohydrates like pizza, pasta, cookies, coke, and cake, you'll want to make more careful food choices.

At times the cause of the sensation of pressure on the chest is ill health. An eight-year-old boy with pneumonia dreamed that a man was standing on his chest holding the whole world. Other people with chest infections or conditions that cause breathing problems have similar dreams. But unless you have a serious chest infection or health condition, or feel pain during your dream, a dream about a weight on the chest or of suffocating probably symbolizes feeling trapped in some waking situation.

Getting Out, Getting Home

A woman who dreamed of being shackled at her wrists and ankles struggled violently to get loose without success. Suddenly she discovered that if she relaxed, she could simply slip free. It was her tension that kept her imprisoned. A man who dreamed of being stuck inside a wall was unable to fight his way through. He realized his efforts were futile, so he relaxed and waited it out until the dream ended. And remember that we can escape from dreams of being trapped in water by discovering underwater breathing.

How can you free yourself from the thing that ensnares you in a dream? Will you find a tool in your back pocket? A key the jailer left behind? Go over your dream, adding the things you need to make it better. If you dream you are caught in branches, nets, ropes, or chains, or are totally paralyzed, try to break loose. Make efforts to move. If your legs feel like lead, see if you can fly; it's sometimes easier. If you can't move your whole body, attempt to move your fingers, toes, or eyes. Send a mental message for help to some rescuer. Or simply relax and wait for it to pass.

When you have a dream of being lost, you feel you have gone astray in waking life. Remind yourself that you can bring what you need into the dream. To be lost is to imply the possibility of rediscovering yourself. Is there a map in your dream pocket? Do you suddenly find a flashlight? A compass? Follow different paths, marking those you have already tried. You might be able to help yourself or get help in bad dreams. You have more power in dreams than you know. Use it.

If you find yourself lost or trapped in a dream, try the above techniques. When you succeed, you are helping to free yourself from the past that has bound you or puzzled you. You can break the spell, find your way, and become free to be yourself.

13

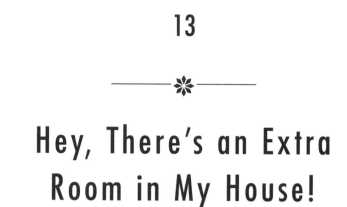

Hey, There's an Extra
Room in My House!

"I discover a hidden staircase between the walls in my house.
When I climb it, I find a treasure connected to my dead
grandmother."

– Zora, 16

To dream of discovering a fantastic new space is one of the delights of
the dream world. You may open a door in your familiar home to find
a whole new room or section of the house that you had no idea was
there. You might be walking in a familiar neighborhood and suddenly
notice an area or a view that you have never seen before. The new space
is always beautiful, amazing, or special in a positive way.

This type of dream is fairly rare, but you are most likely to have it
when you feel that a new part of you or your life is opening up. Your
dreaming mind is shouting, "I've found something wonderful!" You will

feel eager to explore the new space you didn't even know was there. Have you met a new boyfriend or girlfriend? Are you exploring a possible exciting career? Are you able to be more open about your personal feelings and thoughts? These are the kind of situations that prompt you to dream about finding new spaces in your life.

If dreams about being lost or trapped or paralyzed come from feelings of confusion and entrapment, dreams about discovering new spaces involve a sense of expansion, exploration, and new possibilities. The area of life that feels enlarged varies from dreamer to dreamer, but all dreams about finding new space involve a sense of wider horizon and fresh opportunities.

❊

To discover a new space in your dream is to
feel that waking life is expanding.

❊

Open Doors and Windows

If you are inside a house when you discover a new space, your dream will almost certainly involve a door or a window or both. When you open that dream door to discover a new room, you are likely to feel that you have a fresh opportunity in the waking world. The space you find may be decorated in ways that express your developing interest.

When you look out a dream window onto an enchanting garden filled with flowers, sunlight, and singing birds that weren't there before, a new possibility has blossomed in your life. Windows in dreams almost always show us our emotional state of mind at the time of the dream. If you look out on a landscape of great beauty, you are probably open to creative prospects at this time.

Expanding Space

If you dream of strolling outside to suddenly come upon a marvelous area, view, or building, you have an inspiring outlook toward some waking situation. New spaces in dreams suggest new emotional growth. A girl who dreamed she found a cave made of ice in her backyard was probably picturing some "cool" new possibility in her waking world. She found it amazing.

In Zora's dream, space expanded to include a magical staircase between the walls of her house. By climbing it she found a unique treasure on the top floor, one associated with her beloved deceased grandmother. She felt she had found a treasure that would enrich her life ever afterward.

In your waking life, you might be developing your understanding of yourself. When kids begin to develop self-knowledge, they are more likely to dream about finding new spaces. Working on understanding your dreams might itself produce the dream of discovering new space. Among people who have been injured or ill, the dream of discovering new space sometimes occurs as they start to recover.

You might be developing a new friendship, following an exciting course of learning, or unleashing a passionate interest in the arts. You'll be discovering formerly unknown parts of you that widen your horizon in dreams as well as the waking world. When you dream of flying through magnificent spaces, it may express your sense of adventure as you explore your expanding life.

As you grow and develop, life will open to you in ways that may seem impossible right now. Welcome the new spaces you find in your dreams. Explore them with joy. You'll be going forward to meet life in all its glory.

14

Touching Other Realities

"My dead cousin comes to me in dreams, not to threaten me but to offer comfort. She talks to me and helps me through hard times or just spends time with me. She comes to me in dreams whenever I call her."

– Nyla, 17

If you have a dream in which someone you loved who has died appears to give you reassurance and comfort, you will probably wake up feeling very strange. These rare dreams often have an element of seeming more real than real. You might feel as if you have truly been in touch with a good spirit.

Unless you have experienced the death of a person close to you at a young age, you probably won't dream about people who have died. How old you are has a lot to do with how likely you are to have a dream like this. Young children dream about scary ghosts and other supernatural creatures. Older kids dream about vampires, zombies, and such other-worldly creatures, almost always in a negative way. Only a few kids of all ages dream about beloved people or pets who have died (7 percent). Adults, however, have more dreams about deceased people (12 percent). Perhaps their longer lives have brought them in contact with more experiences of death. This means that you are more likely to have this type of dream as you grow older and more experienced.

Although dreams about the dead are not common, they are some-times life-changing for the dreamer. Dreams about the dead may be painful, with scenes of suffering, guilt, or fear. At other times, people have dreams about the dead person that inspire them to go on living, to reinvest joyfully in life, feeling the guidance and love of the lost person. Such dreams sometimes bring a belief in afterlife.

Spooked by a Spirit

If you should have a frightening dream about a person who died, don't worry; it's natural. Sometimes people feel afraid that the dead person is still suffering, especially if they saw the person spend a long time sick or if the death was violent. This can result in dreams about the dead person still being in bad condition. Sometimes people feel abandoned by the person who died; they may have angry dreams about them. Sometimes people wish the person were still alive and dream that they are, that their death was a mistake or a trick. Kids might feel guilty about the death of a parent, as if their behavior somehow caused or contributed to the death; they may have dreams in which they feel blamed. All these reactions to a death are normal and may help dream-ers work through their feelings of grief.

Guided by a Spirit

If you have a comforting dream about a deceased person you loved, it can be a precious gift. Like Nyla, whose dream begins this chapter, you may treasure your dream experiences.

One twelve-year-old girl has recurrent dreams about her dead grandmother standing by a tree in her yard. In other dreams they do together the things they used to do. These dreams feel like a loving visit and make the dreamer feel watched over and protected. A girl who mourned the loss of her pet cat, a companion for nearly four years, was helped by dreams about her animal friend. The girl was going through difficult times that seemed to her unbearable. Then she dreamed her cat was watching over her, lying beside her on the bed as she used to do. She felt this dream of her pet's spirit saved her life. Other kids, too, have dreams of comfort involving a pet they had loved.

We can't know whether the figures in these dreams are actual contacts with another reality or the dreamer's inner self helping to overcome and heal grief. But wherever they come from, these dreams are welcome.

Dreams Beyond Death

Some kids dream about the death of a person close to them the same time that the death takes place. A boy dreamed his grandfather appeared and waved good-bye to him. The next morning he learned of his grandfather's death. It seems to some dreamers that the dying person comes to say good-bye.

A girl dreamed of watching television with her dead brother. In the dream, she changes channels by putting a number with a decimal into the remote control. Suddenly, the screen has dots everywhere, and the dreamer thinks it looks cool. Was the "changed channel" an expression of a different reality? Whether or not dreams can take us to a different reality beyond death, dreams like this give many dreamers a different idea of the meaning of death.

If you have dreams in which you feel guided and guarded by a spirit, you will have had a very special dream experience. Whether the lost loved one is a grandparent or parent, a brother or sister, a cousin or friend, or an adored pet, you will feel cherished and protected. This kind of dream is a blessing.

15

Be a Dream Detective

What are the most important things you need to be your own dream detective?

- good sleep
- good dream recall
- tools for good dream detecting

You'll find the essential kit here.

Good Sleep

You won't have many dreams to work with if you don't get a decent night's sleep. Although your body needs more sleep as you grow, your lifestyle can make this difficult. Homework, sports activities, social gatherings, household chores – these can make sleep too short or too restless. Between the ages of 13 and 19, you will average between seven and eight hours sleep per night, but your body needs about nine hours to function at its best. Experts agree that there are some behaviors that will increase the quality of your sleep.

1. Keep a regular schedule. As much as possible, go to bed and get up at about the same time. This usually isn't convenient on weekends, but the closer you can come to it, the more your body can count on unwinding or gearing up at the same time.

2. Practice healthy habits. Get some exercise during the day. Eat nutritiously in reasonable amounts. Avoid caffeine and sugar after dinnertime, otherwise you'll feel perky when you need to go to bed. Alcohol, nicotine, and drugs really mess up anyone's sleep and dream cycles.

3. Follow a going-to-bed routine. Brush teeth, wash face, read – whatever works for you. This signals your body to get ready to let go.

4. Prepare to sleep well. Keep your bedroom dark, cool but comfortable, quiet, with good air circulation. Some kids like the sound of a fan, air purifier, or white noise machine to drown out small sounds in a steady hum.

5. Make a dream-worthy bed. Cozy bedclothes and pillows with a texture and degree of firmness that's just right for you make getting in bed a pleasure.

6. Go to bed when you're sleepy. Sleepiness comes in waves about every ninety minutes. When your eyes begin to droop, grab that wave to dreamland. Reading a few more pages or watching the next TV show can push you into a later cycle, and leave you sleep- and dream-deprived next morning. Sleep deprivation not only feels bad but can be dangerous if you drive.

7. Let your mind drift off to sleep with pleasant thoughts. Imagine a serene scene at the seashore, in a park, or wherever you feel easy and relaxed . . .

8. Get full light in the morning. After you get up, put yourself in full light as soon as possible. Turn on the electric lights and check the outside weather. Light signals your brain to get ready for the day's activities.

Good Dream Recall

Even if you already keep a dream journal, you may find some new tips in this list, especially number 4.

1. Prepare to dream. Before you go to sleep, put a notepad with a pen clipped to it within easy reach of your bed. Some kids like to use a computer to record their dreams. Others prefer speaking into a tape recorder. If it seems like too much of a commitment to record each night's dreams, at least make notes on the strongest and most powerful ones. Eventually you'll want a written record to get the most from your dreams.

2. Dedicate a special journal to your dreams. You can use a three-ring binder so you can add pages after the dream description. In permanent form, your journal can be handwritten pages or computer printouts. Some kids like to make sketches of special dream images in their journals.

3. Clear the day's activities. Before turning out the light, take a few minutes to write a brief description of what happened during the day and how you felt about it. These events often influence the dreams that follow. By writing what actually went on, you'll be able to separate waking events from dream plots.

4. Make brief notes of any dream recall. In the morning when you wake, or during the night after a dream, make brief notes of any dreams you recall, jotting down key words or phrases. Try to keep your eyes shut, since dream recall is easier this way. (This is why you need writing materials near your bed!) Also try to remain in the body posture in which you awoke while you remember a dream. If you have no dream recall in that position, roll gently into any other sleep position you use. This will often trigger further dream memories. Strangely, recall seems to be attached to the sleep position in which you had the dream. If you have to get up for any reason, and have time, resume your sleep position to see if there are more dream memories. You may not be able to do this on a school morning. If not, pick a weekend, holiday, or vacation to focus on your dreams.

5. Sharpen dream recall. You can improve dream recall by letting your-self sleep in and wake up naturally. You'll be waking up directly from a dream. You dream about 20 percent of the time you are asleep. The final dream of the night lasts about a half-hour. There's plenty to remember if you don't hop out of bed and get distracted. With your eyes closed, let your mind roam to what you were thinking about as you woke up. There's usually a thought, a feeling, or an image. Write this down. This will start the habit of dream recall. You can also try imagining the faces of your family and friends – sometimes this will trigger a dream memory if the person was in your dream. Watch for sudden dream recall during the day when a small thing may bring back a dream. Some people recall dreams best after a nap. Others notice dream memories as they start to drift off the next night. Jot down whatever comes to mind on your dream pad, in brief phrases or sentences. Dream recall is a learned skill, and if you practice you will soon master it.

6. Make a permanent record. Whenever you have time, the next morning or later, copy over your rough dream notes into a computer or journal. You might want to leave wide margins for sketches of odd or strange images and to jot down associations you have to images and words, especially names of people or places you might not recognize months or years later. As with all personal papers, you'll want to keep your dream records in a safe private place.

7. Keep your journal as a valuable dream resource. You'll be making a historical record of your inner life. From this special document, you'll learn your unique dream language. You'll be alerted to when you need to safeguard your health or watch out for trouble on the horizon. You will gain insight into how you really feel about some person or situation. You'll know when you're on the right path or the wrong one. You'll discover ideas for creative projects. And what's more, you'll have fun.

Tools for Good Dream Detecting

Okay, time to put on your Sherlock Holmes cap and cape. You've just had the craziest dream and it makes no sense whatsoever. Actually, it does, but you're too close to see it. You need to step back a little and hunt for the clues that are lying all over the place. Then follow those clues until the dream-mystery unravels.

There are hundreds of ways of working with dreams and thousands of books explaining how to use them. This is my favorite approach to being a dream detective.

1. Describe your dream in the present tense. This will help you get back into the emotions you felt at the time of the dream. It also helps defuse anxiety about a bad dream. Here's an example from the dream journal of fifteen-year-old Lisa (you might recognize this dream from chapter 1 "Oh No, It's After Me"):

> I am looking out the window in my room toward the corner. A boy and a girl are walking up the road hand in hand. Suddenly a whip cracks and they separate. Standing between them is a tall masked stranger.
>
> He sets off firecrackers and cracks spark from his whip. A bunch of rubbish catches on fire. I yell at Daddy through the window to notice the fire but he does not.
>
> Then Dad, Mom, and I are sitting out by the fountain. Tar and building materials are all around. Mother says something about "He is going to the death house to die." I start to ask who she means, Dad or the tall masked stranger, but I wake up and never do find out.

2. What is this dream about in general? Forget the details for the moment. What happened? Use "someone," "somewhere," or "something" instead of specific names, places, and things. But use the right action word. This step is equivalent to solving a crime in which

"Someone murdered someone." The identities of the victim and the murderer may be unknown, but the action – murder – is clear.

In the sample dream, "Someone or something separates a couple." The action word is *separates*.

3. *What was the mood in your dream?* Was it creepy and dark? Did you feel sad? Terrified? Was it bright and sunny? Did you feel adventurous? Was it exciting? Was it mysterious? Did you feel in touch with another world? The setting in your dream often reveals your emotional mood at the time of the dream. Are you in a dangerous area of the city on a dark night? Are you driving through a snowstorm over icy roads? Are you in a sweltering desert? Are you in outer space?

In the sample dream, the setting was Lisa's bedroom, near her home, and in the garden by the fountain. The mood was normal until the masked stranger appeared. Then she felt puzzled.

4. *Who are the characters in your dream?* Now, get out your magnifying glass. The characters in Lisa's dream are three known people (father, mother, and dreamer), and three unknown people (a boy, a girl, and the masked stranger). Is the dream really about these people or is it what they represent? You need to ask a few questions: What kind of person is X (any known dream character)? How is X different from other similar people? What's special or unique about X? If your answer gives you a tingle of recognition, you may be hitting a clue to the meaning of your dream. You need to get the identities and qualities of the key people in your dream.

In Lisa's dream, the father does not notice or ignores the fire she wants him to put out. Lisa thinks of her father as the person who should protect her from danger. In the dream, he does not. Perhaps Lisa feels she's not doing a good job of protecting herself. Her mother is the person she is in conflict with. Lisa's mother had recently started to be more critical and controlling of Lisa. In the dream, the mother predicts death for a man, but it's unclear which one. Death in dreams usually means something is simply "not functional." Which would cease to exist, the protective function (seen in the father) or the mysterious unknown passion (seen in the masked man)? The fire is also a character in the sense that it plays an important role in the dream. The sparks from the masked stranger's whip set fire to rubbish, and the fire could endanger the dreamer's house.

If the dreamer of this dream was a boy – call him Lawrence – his associations would be totally different, depending on his relationship to his father and mother. He might say his father is a nice man, but leads a boring life. He might see his mother as controlling.

5. What is the meaning of bizarre characters, people, or animals, or things that don't exist? Take a blank sheet of paper and in the middle write or sketch the unusual image from your dream. In the sample dream, this would be the mysterious masked stranger. In your dreams it could be a strange person or something totally imaginary. Draw a small circle around that image or phrase. Then draw a larger circle, leaving space to write. Finally draw a third circle with space to write that encloses the other two. (You'll end up with three concentric circles.) Now think about the image or phrase in the center circle. What experiences have you had with anything like it? In the second circle, jot notes on your personal associations. In the third circle, put any cultural associations it might have, such as references to movies, books, films, and so on. Look over what's in the three circles for any similarities.

Lisa associated the boy and girl walking hand in hand with herself and her boyfriend, Don. But who was the masked stranger who separated them? She drew a sketch of him with his long black cape, black clothing, black mask, and whip. During the dream she thought of him as "the tall, masked stranger." She had seen an old movie called *The Scarlet Pimpernel*, and associated the dream figure with the hero of that film – that went in the second circle. "Tall, dark, and handsome" is a phrase used by fortunetellers to refer to a future lover – that went into the outside circle.

Lawrence might see the tall, masked stranger as Zorro, the masked hero from the TV series and the movie with Antonio Banderas. Lawrence could say that the masked stranger leads an adventurous life, rescuing people, and doing good deeds, yet is free to roam open spaces.

Lisa's associations are mainly romantic; Lawrence's are mainly adventurous. So the same dream will have different meanings for them.

6. If this image could talk, what would it say? Give the strange image from your dream a voice and listen to what it says.

Lisa imagines the masked man would say something like, "I'm the unknown, the mysterious part of life you don't know yet. I control the sparks of romance. I'm powerful and dangerous." At the time of this dream, Lisa had been dating for only a few months, and Don was her first boyfriend.

When Lawrence gives the masked stranger a voice, it says, "I'm the life of fun and adventure. I go where I wish and no one tells me what to do. I help people when I decide to and leave when I want to go. I'm free and happy." Lawrence could also have been dating, but would probably be less interested in being part of a couple, fearing it would trap him.

7. Find a central theme in your associations and imaginary conversation with the image. Your image and associations may be linked by many qualities.

In Lisa's dream, the linking qualities are mystery, adventure, power, and danger.

If the dream had been Lawrence's, the linking qualities would have been adventure, fun, and freedom.

8. Return to your dream description and substitute the meanings to the clues you've decoded. Now you've got the clues you need. You know the identities of the characters, what happened, what you did, and how it ended. You can solve the mystery. You need to go through the dream sentence by sentence, filling in these meanings.

I am looking out the window in my room toward the corner.
Translation: I become aware of something coming.

A boy and a girl are walking up the road hand in hand.
Lisa's translation: My boyfriend and I seem to be joined.
Lawrence's translation: My girlfriend is tying me down.

Suddenly a whip cracks and they separate.
Translation: But suddenly we are separated from each other.

Standing between them is a tall masked stranger.
Lisa's translation: Something mysterious, unknown, and dangerous – but romantic – divides us.
Lawrence's translation: Something adventurous and exciting comes between us.

He sets off firecrackers and cracks sparks from his whip.
Lisa's translation: This dangerous but romantic element can make things happen.
Lawrence's translation: This adventurous element can make things happen.

A bunch of rubbish catches on fire (and may spread to house).
Lisa's translation: The part of me that is already affected is not important, but the results could endanger me.
Lawrence's translation: The part that's caught fire is small but I want more.

I yell at Daddy through the window to notice the fire but he does not.
Lisa's translation: I try to alert the protective part of myself to act, but it ignores me.
Lawrence's translation: The part of me that's like my father is boring and ignorant of adventure.

Then Dad, Mom, and I are sitting out by the fountain.
Lisa's translation: In a cool restful space, I contemplate the situation, considering the protective part of me and the critical part of me.
Lawrence's translation: I consider the differences between married life and adventurous life.

Tar and building materials are all around.
Lisa's translation: The raw materials for building something are available.
Lawrence's translation: I want to build a different life from what my family has.

Mother says something about "He is going to the death house to die."
Lisa's translation: The critical part of myself judges that something will cease to exist.
Lawrence's translation: I can't have adventure and be part of a couple at the same time.

I start to ask who she means, Dad or the tall masked stranger, but I wake up and never do find out.
Lisa's translation: Will the protective part of myself stop working, or will the part that has awakened my wish for greater romance stop? I'm not sure.
Lawrence's translation: Will the boring part of life survive, or will I get to have freedom and fun? I don't know yet.

9. Put what you've learned into a short sentence or phrase.
This might take some time, because you'll have to figure out all the details that are less important, to focus on one main point.

For Lisa's dream, it might be "I feel the stirring of romance, but want to protect myself from harm." For Lawrence, it might be "I feel a strong desire to be free of an ordinary life and experience adventure." Both would be expressing a wish to change current life.

10. Think about ways you can approach this goal in the waking state.
Now you've got a simple, straightforward message from your dreaming mind to your waking mind.

The sample dream led Lisa to proceed more slowly in her relationship with Don. Soon she was dating other boys.

Lawrence's dream seemed to tell him to concentrate on ways to make his future involve more exciting adventure. He paid more attention to his enjoyment of sports, and thought about how he could prepare to be an airline pilot, to better fulfill his wish for an adventurous life.

Lisa and Lawrence moved in different directions, based on their personal associations to the same dream images.

Your dreams can help and support you in each step of your life. They teach you what you are feeling at a specific moment in time. The dream journal you start tonight can become a lifetime guide. Close your eyes, open your heart, and listen to your dreams. They're talking to you. May your journey be filled with joy.

About the Author

Patricia Garfield is a worldwide authority on dreams. A clinical psychologist, she has been studying dreams professionally for more than thirty years. She taught college-level courses on dreams as well as courses on psychology for many years.

Dr. Garfield's first book, *Creative Dreaming*, is considered a classic. A best-seller when it was first published in 1974, it has been in print continuously ever since and has appeared in thirteen foreign languages. She also wrote and illustrated *Pathway to Ecstasy: The Way of the Dream Mandala*; *Your Child's Dreams*; *Women's Bodies, Women's Dreams*; *The Healing Power of Dreams*; *The Dream Messenger: How Dreams of the Departed Bring Healing Gifts*; and *The Universal Dream Key: The 12 Most Common Dream Themes Around the World*.

One of the six cofounders of The Association for the Study of Dreams, Dr. Garfield served as the president from 1998 to 1999. She has recorded her own dreams for more than fifty years, keeping what is perhaps the longest dream journal in existence.

You might want to check out the author's website: www.patriciagarfield.com